AF405301

Holding Light

Holding Light

Rebecca Boedges

CONTENTS

Dedication

To all my friends and family who have sat with me through the darkness, fed my soul when I wasn't sure there was a purpose, danced with me (especially my Nia community), and kept me sane – I am forever grateful. To my momma, who has grown with me so much and is the first to get behind every crazy idea I have, my late father who would have been so happy to see this finally published, and supported Mark's art relentlessly often buying paintings to show his admiration for his talent, to my bestie Searsy, the one who first just kept telling me over and over to start writing ten years ago and who is still always willing to pick of the phone or drop a line to process life's latest bullshit or brainstorm some new outlandish business idea – and lastly, Mark, my dear Mark. Our journey has been so full and hard, but here we are, we get to stand in our full light. You have always believed in me, and we have done all of this together. I would not want anyone else by my side, and I'm so proud of you....and us....from a dingy converted garage in Boulder to our sweet, expansive life in Vermont. To my girls, one day, I hope you get to read this and know how much Mommy and Daddy wanted you to be here with us, but also that you two had a spiritual journey that perhaps began long before Mom and Dad had their dreams. And to all the dreamers out there who may be willing to take a chance on this story, we made the impossible come to life, which means you can too!

Omen of the Owl
Whoosh
Soulful wings slice the silence
Golden gaze taps my knowing
Staring into the future
She came to take her home
-R.Boedges

1

Journal Entry

December 30, 2011: Nineteen days past ovulation (DPO)

The amount of pregnancy acronyms is on par with learning a new language. "Nineteen DPO" translates to four weeks and four days of pregnancy. Sitting down to write, I get a pit in my stomach, looking at the numbers for measuring how pregnant I really am—only four weeks and four days? This number is still a conservative estimate, because you get two weeks for free. Pregnancy dating starts from the first day of your last period, but conception usually happens mid-cycle, so at four weeks pregnant, a little fertilized egg has only been in existence for two weeks at best. Who comes up with this shit anyway? So technically, my embryo is two and a half weeks old. How am I going to get through nine months? Or is it ten?

I wish my story began nineteen days ago with our first scheduled intrauterine insemination (IUI), but it didn't. Our baby journey started back in 2008, three long years ago. Everything I have been through up until now is still inconceivable (no pun intended). The only way I can explain it is that I haven't lived through those days, months, and years all together; I have just lived through them one minute and then another at a time. Sometimes all I can do in any given second is breathe and then tell myself that breathing is all I am responsible for, a breath or two. My experience distilled to the involuntary act of inhale, exhale.

How am I going to live through this pregnancy this time? Having babies is a whole lot of waiting, and after all that I've been through, it is like being on an airplane with a blown engine, wrangling the oxygen mask, holding my breath, tucking, bracing, wondering if I am going to land safely, and trust me, I hate flying as it is. Every heartbeat feels like I can't possibly stand being in my own skin for one more second because I might just die from fear. Has anyone ever died from fear? I wonder. I read a study somewhere that babies in orphanages die at higher rates when they are not held. Being held by another person helps newborns regulate their nervous system because they can't regulate their own heartbeats or body temperatures. As babies, we need touch and connection for survival, and without it, we die, so I guess technically I could die from fear if I were a baby, but I'm not. I'm a mom. Or am I?

#

My mind wanders back to my current situation, and at this instant, I'm managing fucking painful Lovenox shots every damn day in the hopes that they help me bring a biological baby into this world. Physical pain is more manageable for me in some ways, although it lights up the same neural net as emotional pain in our nervous system. It's weird to think about; the wiring in my body responds the same to Lovenox shots as it does to sadness, grief, and other painful feelings.

My husband gives me an agonizing Lovenox shot, a blood thinner, every morning in my leg. On recommendation from one of a handful of specialists we have seen on our baby journey, I was tested for Factor V Leiden, and it was positive. I also learned I have a protein S deficiency. Both factors increase my body's blood clotting reaction, but these issues are tangentially related to having children, at best. I am thirty-five times more likely than a woman without this gene mutation to have a blood clot when taking things like the birth control pill that increase estrogen. When I went to see the hematologist, she said, "Oh, and you took Yasmin for fifteen years for birth control? That is like the one birth control pill that has been shown to cause clotting and strokes in women with Factor V." Greaaaat

As a result, she gave me a controversial prescription for daily Lovenox to take during my next pregnancy to thin my blood, decrease the chances of a blood clot, and increase blood flow through the placenta, which may improve pregnancy outcomes. "May" is the key. Every doctor I consulted had a differing opinion; many said the shots won't help, and taking them is worthless. So here I am, taking my injections with a couple of low-dose aspirin daily. I just bought new ski gear this year and a pass, but guess what? No physical activity that might increase the risk of significant injury, because I could hemorrhage and bleed to death. Is this starting to sound a little extreme?

I think so. I realize many people go to great lengths to have children, but every morning when I get my shot, I wonder if this is just taking it too far. I am taking a substance that, were I to sustain a head trauma, could cause life-threatening injuries, and I am doing all of this voluntarily. I am dancing on a line right now of what I think is a reasonable intervention to have children. What is this drive? This pull to keep going? Risking my well-being?

All in hopes that, as I write this, it will somehow have a different outcome than the others. What if somewhere in week twenty, I find out this treatment isn't working, and the same thing is happening? Or some other tragic birth defect? I pray every day that this story is about hope, perseverance, and the power of the human spirit with a happy ending. As I write, I think, am I jinxing myself? Stop thinking those thoughts!

We began by putting the injections in my stomach, as recommended, because the medication goes just below the skin. On the fifth day of getting a shot, I thought, *There is no way I can do this every day for nine months,* as I walked around the house trying to shake out the two hundred bee stings pulsating at the injection site. We then consulted the nurse about more humane locations, and she recommended the upper leg. I seriously wouldn't put my pets through this for the sake of prolonging life; they are that bad. The dreaded morning ritual begins with "MB, can you give me my shot?"

I drop my pants and rub the alcohol in a bull's eye around a spot that is not too bruised on my upper leg. The shots leave big, dark circles in their wake. My husband flicks the needle a few times to move the air around and then says, "Where we goin'?" and I pick a spot by pointing to it.

I turn my head, he squeezes my leg, I say "Ow" from the grip and then begin singing, like a thirty-three record played on forty-five speed: "Wewishyouamerrychristmas, wewishyouamerrychristmas, wewishyouamerrychristmas, andahappynewyear." Then it is done. Until tomorrow.

#

I went in for my second blood draw this morning. The first one was on December 28th to check my Human Chorionic Gonadotropin (hCG) levels, a hormone that rises in early pregnancy. Happy New Year, right? I got a positive home pregnancy test on December 22nd, which was pretty early, ten DPO to be exact. Motherhood began with mastering numerous acronyms as part of the expectant mom role, scouring blogs, reading about other moms-to-be. Somehow knowing I'm not alone in my journey, reading others' stories is timber for my fire of hope. The nurse called me twice on the 28th to let me know that everything looked good and that I needed to retest my hCG on Friday (today).

I am now considered high risk from all of our losses, and this pregnancy, the result of a fertility treatment (IUI), is monitored extra closely. I'm on pregnancy number four, no live births. So, in some ways, these blood tests are pointless. They confirm pregnancy and that the hormone levels are increasing, but there is nothing to be done if they aren't changing as expected. A big realization in this process is that Western medicine does not know much about making babies. All the doctors can do is monitor me very closely until the baby is viable outside of the womb, and then take the little nugget early if necessary. They can monitor growth, hormone levels, and blood flow, but if they discover that one of these things is amiss, then they just monitor more closely. Considering that I have not taken antibiotics since college, getting shots daily and having frequent doctor visits are a shock to my system, maybe even traumatic. Every visit starts to become scarier, and I wait for the bad news before it comes, like watching the hurricane hit your vacation spot a week before you arrive, and upon arrival, you find your beach condo has been washed out and the beach destroyed. You know what is coming, and yet it is still shocking and sad when you see it all close up.

So today, I wait—wait for the nurse to call and tell me the results. The results that may show increased hCG levels indicating a growing pregnancy or a drop in levels predicting an expected loss. Either way, there is nothing to be done. The sad part is that even if she calls and says, "Your levels look great," I remind myself that we are four weeks and four days past ovulation. We have thirty-two weeks and three days left to full term if I go full term, which, depending on the situation, may not be likely.

#

On Wednesday, I waited an hour in the midafternoon in the lab to get my blood drawn, which felt depressing. To avoid the wait today, I went to the lab early in the morning to skip the possibility of a reception area full of people. I wanted to avoid the wait in general, but really, I can't ever hide from the waiting. I never can. I went in at 7:30 a.m., and by 4 p.m., I still had not gotten a call from the nurse reassuring me that my levels look great. So, I called to check in, opting to be more proactive about this pregnancy than I was in the past. I spoke with the nurse, and she began by telling me that she saw the article in the paper about my husband's art and our new gallery. She said she passed it around the office and to our reproductive endocrinologist (RE). At that point, I knew the news was bad. Otherwise, she would have just told me the results. In my mind, I am thinking: *Okay, great, but give me the numbers!*

She then said, "Well, your hCG level measured 375, which is not double the original amount that was 212." She told me that my levels should be doubling every forty-eight hours.

I looked to my husband to do some quick math: 375 - 212 = 163; 163 / 212 = 77 percent. He said that was an increase of more than 70 percent, and I relayed that to the nurse.

She then asked, "Well, is it over 50 percent?"

I said yes.

"Let me check with the doctor about what to do, and I will call you back."

The nurse called back and said that I needed to make a special trip to the clinic on Sunday, January 1st, to get retested, precisely forty-eight hours after my latest test. I asked if going in to get my blood work seven hours earlier on Friday than I did on Wednesday, only forty-one hours in between blood draws versus forty-eight hours, could have affected the results. She replied, "Yes, but that is in the past now. Come in on Sunday morning at 8:30 a.m. to retest." Lesson learned: More info is not always helpful.

Hanging up, I scoured the internet, looking for more information about hCG levels and early pregnancy. Most of what I could find said that hCG levels should double every forty-eight and seventy-two hours. I even discovered a little calculator online to check my rate based on the two readings and the time in between (I thought that was pretty resourceful), and it came out to doubling faster than every forty-eight hours. If I can Google this friggin' calculator, why can't the doctor's office? Google is like a fair-weather friend, though; sometimes, the results are reassuring, but most of the time, horrifying. A symptom could be nothing at all, or I could be dying of cancer. Through my pseudomedical research, I found that the hCG rate of increase matters, not the actual numbers. Shouldn't a doctor's office have this tool on their desktop? This was all comforting. Nonetheless, Sunday's visit loomed.

#

January 1, 2012: Four weeks, six days past ovulation

The first of the year began with a special trip to the hospital at 8:30 a.m. Everything was closed, including the lab where I get my blood drawn, but I had to get my hormone levels checked for the third time. Again, here we are gathering more information, but for what, really? My husband and I waited for the one phlebotomist working on New Year's

Day to come up to the clinic. They called me in, and I took a seat. The nurse I spoke with on Friday came by and said, "Sorry about Friday. I had two other people come to help me with my math. I think you are fine, your numbers were fine, but you would need to retest anyway, so thanks for coming in." What?! On Friday, she had said that they did not know what to make of the results, and they were unclear, and now she says everything looks fine. Forty-eight hours of unnecessary track covered by my high-speed worry train. Arg! I have got to find a way to detach from everything the nurses and doctors report. I tend to hang on to every word that the medical professionals say about my pregnancies, like a moth to a flame, moving toward the words like they will save me from my dark fear and then being burned by them when they potentially reveal no baby this time. There is no way through this experience except riding on the roller coaster of desperation, hoping for a different outcome than before. And my ride has yet to end. As my husband said, the numbers are what the numbers are, whether we test them or not, and there is nothing to be done either way. Happy fucking New Year.

I asked the phlebotomist how he picked phlebotomy. I have seen three of them in the last five days and have been wondering how people choose to work with needles and blood all day. He had an Eastern European accent and looked like a British rock star. His answer was interesting or maybe just pleasantly distracting. He fell into the work in a way. He said that he used to drive a Red Cross truck for a mobile unit and enjoyed the crew, was around blood all day, and it didn't bother him. After a while, he had noticed that it took a certain amount of skill and attention to detail to be a good phlebotomist and that a lot of them were bad. He thought he could be good at the job, so he asked his supervisor, who allowed him to go through the six-month Red Cross training, and that was it. His needle entry was fantastic, by the way; it didn't hurt a bit. I think he is right; it does take a certain amount of attention to detail to be good at phlebotomy. Who knew? I guess we all have our gifts, and thank goddess for those that are drawn to work with blood and needles. I couldn't do it. I can't even give myself a subcutaneous shot daily.

But I guess many people say that about being a therapist, too, and it just comes as second nature to me.

#

Hopefully, she calls soon. I don't want to spend my whole day waiting for the nurse with minimal math skills to contact me. My husband says, "Don't throw her under the bus; she is just doing her job." Ah, he is always the voice of calm, uncritical reason, unless we are talking about his art. I think that may be part of the issue. Since our consultation with a high-risk specialist last year, after delivering our daughter and a visit to Reproductive Endocrinology this past fall, I have not seen or spoken with a doctor throughout this process. I have been put on Lovenox injections, Clomid, hCG trigger shots, and IUI, all of which have been administered by nurses. Every visit is a new health practitioner, and I wonder how this affects pregnancy outcomes. If we know that the relationship is the single most crucial variable in predicting people getting better in therapy, how does the relationship with doctors in Western medicine get neglected so easily? Managed care dictates visits and treatment as much as anything, and insurance companies do not care about the relationship between doctor and patient. I think this shift in medicine affects potential healing and outcomes.

IUI is a funny thing. It is designed to take the guesswork out of conception; the medical community distilled baby-making into basic steps. At the exact right time of the month, day, and hour, I was in the bathroom at the art gallery, and Mark gave me the trigger shot that stimulates ovulation. Then within the next forty-eight hours, Mark had to deliver a sperm specimen to Reproductive Endocrinology. Within a few hours after that, I went to Reproductive Endocrinology to make sure I had eggs ready to release on my ovaries. The trigger shot makes a woman produce a few eggs, which is why there is a risk of multiple babies with IUI and IVF. My ovaries looked ready, so I had a turkey baster injected into my yoni, and there you have it! So romantic! The process from start to finish is so stressful because of the specific timing, and it is so disembodied. It makes my stomach turn. The success rate quoted to us was around a 10 percent chance of conception, and the bill was around twelve hundred dollars. I wonder to myself how baby-making is affected when we've taken all the fun out, which is putting it kindly; it's more like dreadful.

#

January 10, 2012: Six weeks, one day past ovulation

On January 1st, a doctor (whom I have never spoken with or met) called me in the afternoon to report that my hCG was 888 and that looked great. She said to call on Tuesday to schedule an ultrasound. I breathed a sigh of relief and went to sleep for a few hours. Even though I knew the nurse from Friday did not know what she was talking about, I still felt this pang of doubt. This pregnancy could just as easily end like all the others. Why would it be different now?

On Tuesday, January 3rd, I called to schedule my ultrasound, and the person at the front desk asked, "Do you need it today or sometime soon?"

I replied, "I don't know. The doctor just said to call on Tuesday to schedule it."

"Who did you speak with?"

I told her the name and said that she was not the one that was managing my case but another doctor.

"Well, she is the one who gave you the test results, so I will ask her." Now, I have repeated my story an unfathomable number of times to doctors and nurses, because each time I see someone new, the person asks that I start from the beginning. So, having a new doctor added on a whim makes my heart skip.

Recalling everything I have endured with every new doctor, nurse, and medical professional is something I begin to prep myself for the night before. Every new appointment is game day, and I have to review the plays in my head: each pregnancy, the outcome, the length of the pregnancy, and the presumed reason it did not thrive. I almost become numb to recounting the medical details, but what never changes is the "Awww" sympathy response from the listener. I generally try to tell myself my story is not that bad, but I can never stay in that denial when I hear the "Awww," and it always comes. Sometimes said medical professional gets tears in her eyes listening to the repeated losses and lack of explanation. That is the worst, really. And I think to myself at that point, *Crap, I haven't even made it to the worst part yet*, and I usually begin to feel nauseated and sweaty. Like saying the words out loud brings the pang of every "I'm sorry, there is no heartbeat" right into the room with us all at the same time, as if my baby story is a black hole abyss that I stand in every time I say the words out loud, and every loss is like each speck of matter and dust sucked into the vacuum pummeling my fragile skin surface with craters of grief and heartbreak.

#

So, the woman at the front desk got off the phone with me and said she would talk to the doctor who called me with my hCG results on New Year's Day. She called back and said, "You need to come in for an ultrasound in two weeks." That's it? I just had to have three blood tests in six days, and now I have to wait two and a half weeks? Ahhhhh! So I booked the ultrasound for January 19th, 2012, when we will find out if there is a heartbeat and what the viability of the pregnancy is. So, now we are just waiting, *again*.

I feel terribly detached from it all at this point, and yet not. We have told some close friends our news, people that will support us no matter the outcome. That is one thing that I have learned through all our losses: the ability to receive support. My friends and family have carried me through.

#

February 18, 2012

I just have not been able to write. On the night of January 17th, I dreamt that I started bleeding and that I was having a miscarriage. In my dream, I was so pissed off. *Are you kidding me? Two days before we go in for an ultrasound? Fuck!* When I woke, I did not want it to be true. I have had so many prophetic dreams in the past that I just wanted this one not to be true. I did not tell my husband about the dream. Instead, I mentioned that I was not having an increase in pregnancy symptoms like nausea, swelling, unrelenting hunger, so I was unsure about the baby's viability. The next evening, the night before the ultrasound, I went to the bathroom, and there was blood. My heart sank. I went downstairs and told Mark. The hardest part about any of this is telling Mark. It is like I have some knowing because it is my body, but he is generally so optimistic. It breaks my heart to see the disappointment in his eyes. I guess somewhere deep, deep, on a cellular level, I am failing my duty as a wife. We are put on this planet to procreate; what if I am a woman who can't have children? And of course, it's me, right? Nothing to do with the combination of us. This pull to have kids is so beyond me at this point.

On January 19th, we headed into the appointment. I was so anxious, I called in sick from teaching my Nia fitness class, which I rarely do unless I am bedridden. I was paralyzed with fear. Could I face this again? We went to the doctor—well, we saw the ultrasound technician—and I asked if we would see a doctor today. The nurse told us that we would after the technician did the ultrasound. She put the device, probe, whatever it is, in, and I knew immediately that she did not see a heartbeat. Every time I go in for an early ultrasound, they have to put in a probe and maneuver it to different angles to get the pictures they need. I have become anesthetized to how many hands, probes, heads have been in, around, and up my vagina at this point. My body is no longer my own in many ways. It is a baby machine that is broken.

The ultrasound technician quickly went from my uterus to measuring ovaries and follicles, probably like she was trained to do. In case there is no heartbeat, do all the other measurements first, so you don't have to put them through it at the end after you tell them their fetus is lifeless.

"I'm sorry, I am only seeing a six-week-old baby here when you should be seven and a half weeks, and there is no heartbeat." I looked at my husband—oooh goddess, those blue eyes, and the ocean of sadness. As I write, I can see them, barely tearing up, so stoic and yet so disappointed. So, so disappointed. Again, my inner critic laments, *Who am I as a wife who cannot reproduce?* I know it is not logical, but my unconscious thoughts arising to the surface are deafening, patriarchal, and archaic.

The doctor came in and expressed her sadness. With so much loss, I thought that she would tell me to forget this idea about having our own biological children, that I am broken. To the contrary, she said that we fall into this category of "unknown," and that what they do know is that the live birth rate is 75 percent. She said, "I think if you can, keep trying."

I asked her, "So for couples in our situation, when you don't have an answer about what is happening, the recommendation is to keep trying, because eventually, the statistics will fall in your favor?"

And she said, "Yes."

Holy cow, this is modern medicine, people! Now I am getting quoted some stats and being told that, because of those odds, I will eventually have a child but could sustain many losses between now and then. Is this good news? I honestly still don't know. How much loss can my body really take?

We left the visit feeling discouraged that things would happen naturally on their own and disheartened that there wasn't much to be done without jumping into costly treatments. We both decided that in vitro fertilization (IVF) at $12,000-$15,000 a try was just too much to ever consider for us. For some people, like one nurse I met, taking out a second mortgage on her house was just a part of having kids with intervention—no big deal. We all have to find our own way.

After that visit, I took a break from journaling. I couldn't take it. What am I going to write about? Our journey to never having children? Heartbreaking and disappointing? We have enough of that in the world; one more story, my story, is just the story of being human, really.

About two and a half weeks ago, I went to the bookstore—a dying breed, by the way—to find something new to read. I picked up a sci-fi novel, which is usually not my thing, and meandered aimlessly, scouring hardcover jackets. I picked up some other paperback, which I can't remember now what it was, and wandered toward checkout. On the way, I passed by a title, *The Hidden Power of Your Past Lives,* by Sandra Anne Taylor. Now, I am pretty open-minded; I went to Naropa University to study body-based psychotherapy and have spent many hours poring over books and research that show this intricate connection between emotional and physical well-being and the ability to self-heal. So why can't I heal myself, right? Why can't I heal whatever is happening so that I can have children? I ask myself the same question every day.

On a whim, a pull, I swapped the second book I picked up for this one on past-life regression with an accompanying CD. Written by a psychotherapist who worked with folks through hypnosis, she shares her experiences of people's memories of past lives.

I personally believe there is something that happens in good therapy that is difficult to name, outside of our understanding of healing, and yet profoundly effective. I call it "being in the soup;" it feels like we are underwater, it gets slow and murky, and words matter less. Psychology experts may refer to this as the unconscious, but I'm not convinced that explains it entirely. I see this day in and day out with my clients; they absolutely inspire me. The soup is generally where a shift happens. So, I thought, ehhh, what the heck. When we got home that night, I started reading through my new purchase, and I could not put it down. The author recommends reading through the whole thing before getting to the CD, but I rarely follow directions, advice, or rules. Just ask Mark about my "best recipes"—totally delectable and never repeatable, because I look at a recipe, get a gist, and then throw in some spices and fairy dust without measuring or thinking, and voila!

I create the space, get comfy, and pop in the CD. I have a lot of experience meditating, so I think I will just roll with it and see what happens. My loving hubby pops his head in and says, "Whatcha doin'?" in his playful way.

"Doing a past-life regression, want to join me?"

He responds with, "Heh, heh, I'm okay" in his *You are a little nutty, but I love you anyway, dear* tone whenever I ask him to try some new kooky thing, like drinking homemade fermented cabbage juice.

Long story, but one time I did try to make my own kimchi in a plastic container, big mistake. Note to self: Only glass containers for making Kimchi. It smelled like rancid wastewater had been used to spray-wash our entire condo. I did pour the juice off and drink it in the name of replenishing my beneficial gut flora, but I almost puked. We had to throw away everything used in the making of this concoction because of the stench, and we aired out our home for a few hours. This should be convincing evidence that I will try almost anything once, especially in the name of healing.

CD playing, I begin my regression meditation. Honestly, expecting nothing, or even if I did get something, how would I know I am not making it up? I don't. The reality is, I just sit into the not knowing, with the intent that it can't possibly hurt. Hey, I survived ill-fermented cabbage juice, right? I mean, modern medicine has given me a statistic as a way to solve our childbearing problem, so sitting and meditating about some karmic pattern can't be that far off.

I sink in easily as the voice guides me to visualize my surroundings. I see myself clearly on cobblestone streets among tall brick buildings. I smell roasting chestnuts, and it is the late 1890s, I think, in New York City. I can still see this image clearly as I write, like a painting I once saw. As I explore my surroundings some more, I look down at my feet, as the voice in my ear directs, and I see these pointy, lace-up, witchy type shoes that look like something Mary Poppins might wear. I am wearing a light blue dress, with a fluffy undercoat and a large hat. I see a woman in the doorway or alleyway, and she approaches me for help. She has a white cloth over her head. I can tell that what she is about to ask me is secretive in nature.

I then flash to meeting a woman, at night, in my husband's office—he was a doctor—where I am explaining her abortion procedure. But she is not just any woman; she is a nun. And now, it becomes clear that I actually helped many women of the Catholic church have abortions. I did this work at night and was trained by my husband.

Then I move to a scene later in life where I am running an orphanage. I come out of the regression and tell my husband everything I have written here. I don't know where all of these details came from, nor do I necessarily believe them, but it makes for a great story, and who knows? Maybe I'm working out some karma from helping babies move in and out of this plane of existence in a past life.

I tell my family about my regression, chatting about the role of women and having children in our culture. I can't tell you how many people will randomly ask me if I have children, yet it has occurred to me that we would never ask such a rude and personal question of an almost stranger such as "Do you have a college degree?" or "How many degrees do you have?" Sometimes I have visions of telling the next person who asks me if I have children, "Yes, and they all died." That is the other weird thing, the whole "mom" definition. I have children who died before birth—am I a mom? Who decides? What about the miscarriages? Are you a mom with no live births? It seems like such a simple question; the answer is yes, right? But then what happens when someone asks you if you have any children, and then you say yes, and then they ask, "How old?" and you say, "Well, they don't have an age because they passed away."

I have mentally had that conversation many times, and the discomfort in such a casual encounter is just not something I am ready to live out every time. And yet, a part of me feels like I am betraying my first daughter's short life by not acknowledging her in casual conversation with strangers.

\#

Today, while in the backyard, walking my dog, sobbing with grief and despair, this voice in my head said, *Write, write, tell this story.* So here I am, writing again; a relentless yearning urges me on.

2

Omen Of The Owl

November 17, 2010

I was driving and had not felt her move in a while, and suddenly she pummeled me, like running feet or something, and I said out loud, "Oh, there you are, I was wondering where you were." That was the last time I felt her move, under the stoplight intersecting Dorset and Williston Roads.

I came home and was so tired but knew I had to take our dog Shelby out for a walk. It was late afternoon in November, and as a way to avoid more fatigue, I put Shelb in the car and went to a favorite dog park nearby. When I got there, there weren't any dogs, so I drove over to the other dog park near our house. There were no dogs there, either. Unbelievable. Four o'clock on a Tuesday afternoon and both dog parks are empty. So, I decided to head home and take Shelby for a walk in the small area of woods near our house. This set of woods is maybe two football fields at most, in the middle of suburban streets, and the airport is less than one mile east of us. We are very close, although not directly in the flight path, but close enough that when the F-16s take off, they rattle our windows, and I can't hold a conversation on the phone due to the noise.

It was still light out, and she and I trotted into the woods. I was dragging my super pregnant body down the trail, and Shelby was running wildly, weaving between brush and trees. It was cool, cloudy, and gray; dusk was rapidly approaching. Our days get very short up here in Northern Vermont as we approach the winter solstice. The smell of musty, rotting, crunchy leaves was in the air, and the crisp chill seared my nostrils. As we rounded the bend in the trail that follows the ravine, maybe one hundred yards from the road, planes above, an enormous something swooped down at eye level in front of my dog and me. It came so close, I thought I could touch it, and I froze in fear. My eyes followed it to the left, and it perched itself on a branch twenty feet away, about eight feet from the ground. My belly gets warm as I remember this moment in the woods. She was huge.

With Shelby right next to me, I then saw that this mysterious creature was an owl, perched with its back to us. I instinctively followed her, causing a raucous with all the crunching leaves and snapping sticks underfoot, knowing at any minute this large nocturnal watcher of the night was bound to take flight because of our approach from behind. To my dismay, she never turned to acknowledge me, even though she could turn her head 270 degrees without moving if she were inclined. I walked right underneath her and looked up; she returned my stare as if she were just waiting for me to come stand at her feet. She was two arm lengths away, and I can still see her eyes: They were beyond human, so intelligent, crystal-clear bronze. Neither one of us blinked. I was looking at her, and she was looking at me. Our souls met; it was like she had X-ray vision into my heart.

Peering into her owl eyes as she sat stoically on that rickety branch—she was enormous, a barred owl, but I did not know that at the time—I am in awe. I think, *Holy guacamole, this bird is making eye contact without flinching, even with my dog by my side.* Her eyes had this knowing, this spirit. Tears started to fall down my cold cheeks, and I started asking her, out loud, "Why are you here? What do you have to tell me?" Again, as I write this, I think, *I am a psychotherapist—do I talk to animals? Am I going crazy? Will I have clients after this?* I don't have a practice of talking to animals in nature, but on that day, I was overcome by her presence and sensed she was a messenger. In that moment, I did not get an answer, or perhaps I couldn't hear it yet, but the truth would reveal itself soon enough.

I talked to her for a good ten minutes while she maintained her unwavering gaze, and my dog continued to run around underneath her branch. After what felt like an eternity, and not really wanting to leave because I felt like she was supposed to leave me first, I turned and retreated, tearful, moved by the power of our meeting. Deep down, I felt like she was trying to tell me something. Walking the few hundred feet back home, I was itching to tell someone about this mystical visit, so I immediately called my mom.

She said, "I know, when you look in the eyes of an owl, there is an intellect there." I told Mark about it as well. He was also amazed that she allowed me to approach her so closely in daylight and made eye contact while I talked to her, even while Shelby was skittering about. The power of her presence was undeniable, and it was as if we knew each other like old friends.

The following morning, November 18th, we went to the doctor because I was uneasy that I hadn't felt our daughter kick in a while. Driving to the visit, I naively said to Mark things like, "I'm probably just overreacting" and "At this point, if something is wrong, at least she can be delivered."

We arrived at the doctor's office. Accustomed to dealing with anxious moms, the nurse brought me into an office to put a monitor on my belly. The laissez-faire attitude of everyone communicated the number of visits they scheduled to reassure new moms that everything is going just fine. The nurse put the strap on my belly to begin the stress test. Silence. The nurse started making excuses for not finding the heartbeat like, "Oh, they sometimes like to hide" and moved the probe along the lower parts of my abdomen where they were likely to find a baby nestled. More silence. The more her searches were met with deafening silence, the more my body started to rush hot and cold, heart racing, head dizzy, feeling trapped and needing to run. And at that exact moment, I was being rushed into the ultrasound room swimming with doctors and nurses. The news traveled quickly that there was an emergency; the staff's approach was no longer "Let's just do a quick check-see." The sense of alarm was contagious.

Shuffled into the large patient room with ultrasound. Wands rapidly searching my little belly. No heartbeat. No movement. I had been in to see the doctor the Wednesday before and measured two centimeters small, expressed my concern, and was told, "Don't worry about it. If you measure small again in two weeks, we will do an ultrasound to check her." There was no two weeks later. I could see her tiny body curled up on the screen on the wall, in the fetal position. It was no longer her, just a body; her soul had taken flight.

The doctor said, "I'm sorry, there is no heartbeat."

Another doctor grabbed the ultrasound wand and exclaimed in an accusatory way, "There is no fluid around this baby," like someone in the room, me included, should have known there was no fluid. No fluid didn't just happen overnight.

I screamed, kicked off my shoes——like they flew across the room, and I can remember someone in there laughing for a second because I flung them so hard—and I shattered into sobs. This could not be happening, not to me, no way. She was just with us; she was just here. I was just playing flashlight belly tag the other night. How did we not know there was no fluid? How did she die? I can't do this. My thoughts begin racing: *I cannot deliver a dead baby. They are going to have to take her by C-section while I am knocked out, oh god, and the phone calls, oh god, how does anyone survive this? This is not happening; this cannot be happening.*

Before I felt ready, everyone started to move me to the door to go home to process the news. I felt rushed, not ready to transition, but before my body and mind had time to agree with my exit, we were walking out the door from our final ultrasound.

I can see that moment so viscerally in my mind's eye and feel it in my body. That is trauma, the flashing hot and cold, the panic, the fear, the doom of what is about to come, the powerlessness. The inescapable powerlessness. I am human, I have a breaking point, and this is it. There is nothing worse; this is it. I am broken.

The pain of that day still resonates with me and comes in waves, even now, a year later. Laying here today sick, I became aware of this deep, entrenched, profound guilt for having caused my daughter's death—guilt that my body failed her and has not supported all the other babies that I have tried to bring into this plane of existence.. There was a problem with the placenta; it did not develop properly. How could I not have realized that she was not moving appropriately? Not enough? How come I did not push the issue when I measured two centimeters small at thirty-three weeks? How, when I had a dream about her premature birth at seven weeks, could I not have done something? On some level, my body has not provided the right host environment for these babies, and they have died. I know this is not rational, logical thought, but this is the acute feeling. The tears flood me like a tsunami, waves of grief crashing their way to the surface, leaving me exhausted and gasping for air. Laying here, my doggie nudging me, I have a swift flash image of helping women abort their children in my "past life." I helped abort babies because I was a helper; my soul now thinks it is helping me. I did not read past the initial regression, so I don't know how to fix the karma yet or work it out, but who knows? This doesn't seem any crazier to me than hoping that the odds will turn in our favor. So, with an openness to not knowing and at the risk of sounding totally crazy, I will write my story. Our daughter would want that; she came to me for a reason, as short as her life was this time.

3

The Beginning Of Us

Boulder, Colorado: 2002

I kept thinking that our story started with Chapter One, when I decided to start writing after some of our losses, but really it dawns at the beginning of us. My husband, Mark, is a professional artist, recognized as one of the best representational landscape artists in the United States, maybe in other countries as well. People collect his work and travel from all over the world to take lessons from him. He mainly paints landscapes as he sees them, rendering as much realism as possible through his oils and somewhat controversial Mongoose-hair brushes. His art is old school, the way the old masters used to paint, in a modern digital age. He takes his canvas and materials outside to paint on location like Monet used to, sometimes hiking a few miles in to catch the light on a mountain lake. Most art programs do not even teach oils anymore or allow them on their campus due to the toxicity of the fumes and concerns around the disposal. In a way, it fits his personality; he always says that he feels like he would have been at home in the fifties; maybe he's an old soul.

Our art pursuit began back in Colorado around 2003. Mark was living out of a converted garage that housed his bedroom, lounge room, art studio, and guitars. His guitar playing was one of the things that melted my heart when we first met—of course, who does not fall for the guitar player?! Anyway, he was working part-time as a web developer and back in graduate school for art at the University of Colorado, Boulder. The program was primarily designed for abstract artists, so while attending, he spent a lot of time out in the mountains, painting from life. They call it "plein air"—that's kind of his thing.

Enamored with his budding talent, I had a hunch that his art was decent. Since I can remember, post-college, I have been dreaming up ways to make money on my own terms. I remember thinking I should scrape together the money to buy an ATM for my apartment building in Denver to make some extra cash. Ha! I told Mark about that recently, and he said, "You know that is one of those ideas that if you had followed through with it in 2000, you might have something now." Well, crap! My million-dollar idea has gotten away from me. Good thing I'm a therapist now.

Around the time that we met, although just a student, I believed Mark's work had promise. Now, why? I can't say for sure, because I literally knew nothing about art, the art business, or the art world. Intuition, based on total lack of expertise, urged me to tell him that I thought he should start selling his work, as if I was some professional art broker or something. Sometimes I have these beliefs or ideas, and I just state them as fact and will them into truth, and maybe there was a little of that going on here—who can say? Like any brooding artist, he told me no way and that his art wasn't good enough. So, being the thrifty go-getter that I am, I decided to pitch his artwork to the 2003 Denver Student Art League's annual art fair held in the late spring every year. The fair is for beginning to mid-level artists and generally posts high sales. It is rather competitive to get juried into the event and designed for amateur artists just starting out in their careers. What did he have to lose? What did I have to lose? If he didn't get in, I wouldn't tell him I pitched his work, and if he did, well, I'd cross that bridge when we got there.

He truly loved what he did when he was doing it; his passion for painting made me a believer. Generally, we just need one of those on our team, but a few is a force. Believers help us find the courage to live our dreams. So I filled out the application (I cringe a little as I write that;

never in a million years would I ever do such a thing now, I mean maybe not) and submitted it without his knowledge. I was young, naive, and drunk with hope. I talk about hope in many ways throughout my story; I guess this was one of the first times hope carried us through. My dad recently told me that we are all entitled to hope no matter our circumstances. Until our last breath, we can hope. I find comfort in this idea and believe that hope tempered with the desire and ability to take significant risks creates a rich life. I knew that they had to let Mark into the show, and they did.

So, next problem: How do I tell him I submitted his application without his knowledge and that now we are on the hook for selling his work at the fair? I approached him gently and broke the news. The time between me saying, "So, I did this thing . . ." and his acknowledgement felt like an eternity. Eventually, his face lit up with delight. Luckily, he was excited. We sat looking at all his artwork, studies, finished works, sketches, He had created over a hundred pieces in the few years he had been painting. If we ever do a retrospective and include scenes sold at that show, I'm sure we would all be amazed. I would be amazed that we have created a business out of art starting from that one decision, he would be amazed that some of his stuff was actually good back then, and then we would be amazed that people bought most of it.

Once I shared the admission with Mark, we quickly moved on to logistics. In the art world, framing is as critical as the work. You cannot hang some shabby frame on a $10,000 painting and hope it sells. That would be like gifting a three-carat diamond ring wrapped in old newspaper; it is just all wrong. Maybe there is a life lesson here about presentation: No matter what I present, wrap it in a bow and a smile.

We were young and clueless, so we spent about a month buying unstained framing wood from the hardware store, stained and finished it (yikes), cut it with a miter saw (double yikes), and then glued it into frames. Imagine the popular commercial hobby store frames rank at about Grade D in quality. Our creations came in at about Grade Z. No joke, bad—like, embarrassingly bad. Thank goddess, we just did not know. Had I known what I know now, I wouldn't have gone to that show, solely because we could not afford the proper framing and the utter embarrassment that would have come from knowing that we were selling fine art wrapped in garbaaage.

Arriving the day of the show, it was sunny and hot, like it is 370 days a year in Colorado, as the joke goes. We began to set up our ten-by-ten outdoor tent, financed on a credit card with hopes that we might be able to pay it off after the show. Some folks had hired help to set up their tents, but we were flat broke, so we stumbled through it on our own. Walls up, what a relief, but then we were staring at boxes of artwork, wondering how the hell we display it. Looking around, I saw these rows of professional tents with elaborate displays and marketing signage; we were definitely out of our league. Adorned with a healthy amount of twine and luck, Mark fashioned a way to hang the fifteen or so pieces that we had so elegantly framed (cough!). My whole body cringes at this part of the story; the memory of shame makes my skin and bones shrink into themselves. Our tent and display arrangement, in the row of white tents and displays, was forgettable, easily overlooked, in the sea of vendors. Bins of unframed studies lined the tables and ground, like a flea market about to open, and our handful of framed paintings showcased wildly, swinging with each breeze, tethered from the inner poles of the tent.

Some of the bin work was just simple, monochromatic studies of flowers. Others were sizeable, finished mountain scenes, including literally every piece of art Mark had painted over the last couple of years. I can remember hanging one painting in particular, depicting the foothills in the background while the foreground consisted of highway overpasses and electrical wires. He had this thing about painting the truth, and the truth was the foothills were congested with detritus of civilization, and he didn't want to distort the view. Sometimes too much truth can get you into trouble, especially in art. I wondered silently, *Who is going to buy this?* But guess which paintings collectors loved most? Bingo! Lesson learned: I can never truly anticipate a market or how much reality is too much.

Our upper-end price point eludes me to this day, but I imagine it was roughly $1,000 on any given painting. Today, Mark's paintings sell for many times that, so I guess you can say we have come a long way! But the road from then until now has been wrought with ups and downs, grief, loss, financial hardship, grad school, moves, real estate debacles, and the list goes on. Yet, somehow, I always kept hoping.

Remember the really shitty framing? Divine intervention had situated Abend Gallery in our aisle, a few tents down from us, and she was selling prefab frames at the show. People were so admiring of Mark's work that they would buy it, carry it a few stops down to Abend, and have it reframed on the spot. Now that I think about it, perhaps that was fate, because Chris, who still owns Abend Gallery, approached us at the end of the weekend, inviting Mark to show in her gallery. Thus, our first collectors, in need of frames, inadvertently pitched Mark's work to one of the most prominent galleries in town. That may have been the best advertising freebie we have ever received.

The day wore on and folks kept coming by and enthusiastically buying Mark's studies and giving him glowing feedback on his art. With every hour, our confidence grew that we were in the right place and that he maybe had a shot at an art career. By evening, our tent was mostly empty, and we had been rewarded for taking such a risk. The next day was a repeat of the first, and at the end of the weekend, we basically sold out.

We sold out! I get so excited when I remember that show; it was one of our first major wins in his career. I think we made a few thousand dollars after everyone got their "cut" (everyone takes a cut in the art world), and that was more money than either one of us had had in our accounts ever in our lives. That was spring, and by summer, Mark took that money, bought me an engagement ring, and asked me to marry him. I did not always imagine myself having children or even being married. I didn't fantasize about my wedding day or imagine my life with a white picket fence and two kids, but when I met Mark, I felt we were meant to be together. I can't explain it. Within a few months of dating, I just had a felt sense that we would get married. It took him a little longer to figure that out, of course.

I said yes, now *we* are at the beginning, saying yes.

4

My First Gut Feeling

Middletown, Connecticut: Early 1980s

I called myself an atheist for many years. Although I was raised Catholic and got confirmed in high school, my mom always reminds me that I am the only one out of her four children that chose to be confirmed. I did not follow through on church, but of course, as all great Catholic mothers do, she has her way of serving guilt on a shiny platter. We all laugh about it when she does it, though, including her.

I have always had an incredible gut feel about people and life that I have mostly honored. My gut is my more profound knowing, and before all of our tragic loss, I did not appreciate how that feeling is actually a connection to the universal divine.

Whenever I have anxiety about a choice, I call upon this feeling to guide me to the right decisions for me in the moment. Our losses have taught me that my intuition, my gut feel, is calling on some universal connection, some other way of knowing and understanding that the mind couldn't possibly comprehend. Maybe goddess Sophia has always been with me, but I discovered her more fully through our daughter. Sophia is the goddess of wisdom, intuitive wisdom, and joy, and her symbol is the owl. I only came to know about her through a friend, after my owl visit. The meaning of the owl continually unfolds for me on an as-needed basis.

My earliest memory of my intuition guiding me is from kindergarten or first grade, while waiting for the bus at the end of our driveway. The driveway extended about five hundred yards from the house to the road. My brother was running late, and my mom had sent me out to wave the bus down to avoid missing it. Usually, our bus approached from the top of the hill down towards our drive, but today, it came from the bottom of the hill, traveling in the opposite direction. The male driver stopped the bus where I was standing, and through his open window, the kind that slides sideways, asked me to get on. I recall him wearing a brown one-piece outfit, like a mechanic. The details are fuzzy, but I got terribly frightened, and I turned and ran up the driveway into my mother's arms as she was coming down with my older brother. She hugged me and continued back down to the bus with us by her side. She talked to the driver for a minute to get the story, then gave some gentle encouragement for me to get on the bus. He said he was "helping out" our elementary school that morning. I wouldn't budge. I absolutely refused to get on the bus and sobbed. My mom told him thanks, but she would take us to school, and waved him on. He continued on route up the street and did not stop for any of the other children waiting at the end of their driveways.

My mom called the "bus department," whatever that is, and they were unaware of who he was and couldn't identify him. I can remember, though, by the end of the day, my brother and I recalled differing descriptions of the driver. I thought he had a beard, Tim said no; I thought he had a brown suit, Tim said he wore something else. Memory is funny like that; it changes over time, especially with a traumatic event. I feared that man and hyperfocused on getting away, not what he looked like.

I believe my little belly kept my brother and me safe that day. She has a mind of her own, that one. If we experience too much trauma early on, we get disconnected from our belly's way of knowing. We actually stop listening to it or literally cannot feel it anymore. One of my professors in graduate school used to call it "instinct injured" when we can no longer sense our gut feel. To survive trauma, we move up out of our bodily sensation, sensing mainly our head and using thoughts to process our experiences, because the sensations are too scary. Sensations can hold memories, and sometimes those memories are overwhelming. We then primarily operate from the neck up, navigating our lives through thinking versus feeling. Lots and lots of thinking, but not a lot of feeling.

Thoughts come from the mind, the prefrontal cortex, to be exact, but feelings come from the ability to decode sensations in the body; sensation is the language of emotion. Our nervous systems can't actually think and feel simultaneously, so if I am thinking, I am not feeling, and vice versa. We can switch back and forth rather quickly with practice, but one clear way I know if I am feeling my feelings is to notice if I am thinking a thought, If I am, then I'm not actually feeling my feelings. Thoughts are only about the future or past, so thinking is a way of not being present. Our culture values thinking over feeling, spending more time in thought than in presence.

Thwarted kidnapping? Who knows, but I spent my childhood afraid of being kidnapped, so on a cellular level, I think that guy was trouble. We are all born with that sense, the deeper knowing, but in Western culture, we are taught that information that can't be proven is false. It leaves knowing the world through a felt sense in some category of its own, and that is me. Call it New-Agey, kooky, clairvoyant, psychic, spiritual, psychotic, mindful; therapist, healer, woman—there are too many labels to mention. All I know is it took me life and loss to get back to that place that I have always known since early childhood. I believe this to be true for everyone, but we are taught through experience and labels to dismiss intuition.

In fact, intuition had a home in medicine and healing long ago. In early Colonial America, women nursed, healed the sick, and birthed babies of family and friends. Women held medical knowledge and passed it down through their female lineage, using natural resources to create medicine. Immigrant women, as well as Native Americans, were the healers of the community. Midwifery was also a decent way for women to make money. Around 1716, New York City began requiring licenses to practice Midwifery. Although the statistics for live births were not recorded accurately, it has been documented that around 90 to 95 percent of births were live before regulations. The current stillbirth rate in the US is about 1 percent, about ten times the rate of babies that die from SIDS, but we always hear about SIDS as new moms. Why?

With the development of hospitals in the mid-1700s and the licensure of doctors around 1765, men began to create a cohesive practice of medicine and discourage local healers from practicing, because they were competition. They did so by claiming local healers were deceitful and practicing "quackery," which ultimately limited financial competition (https://www.midwiferytoday.com/web-article/history-midwifery-childbirth-america-time-line/). Medicine has always been a business. Requiring licenses meant that formal education was necessary to practice, and most women were illiterate and did not have the time or money for school. Essentially, regulations limited women's access to continue practicing medicine, and it became a male-dominated field that limited training to mostly wealthy men who could afford it. Ironically, a male doctor opened the first formal training center for midwives. And through making education exclusive and unaffordable to women is one of the ways that the patriarchy took over medicine, moved it to books, and into the cognitive realm. Research dictates fact and practice from this point on.

Of course, there are so many benefits to modern medicine, but there are also many gifts of intuition. I imagine that this turn in history put the answers to healing in textbooks, out of our own feminine intuitive bodies, and into the heads of men. We gained experts and lost healers. The latest trauma research, led by men, demonstrates efficacy in substance-assisted therapy using MDMA and ketamine, using altered states to promote healing (For example: https://www.ptsd.va.gov/understand_tx/mdma_assisted_therapy.asp). Although effective, I'm sure, at the last conference I attended, I was left with this nagging feeling that we now, in Western medicine, are coming back to what indigenous cultures have known forever: Music, dance, rhythm, substances, and ritual create altered states that heal the body/mind. Research is bringing us back to the traditions we have destroyed through colonialism. We all have the innate ability to self-heal some things, and we need our connection to our own intuition to tap into it, not the advice of an expert.

5

When A Calling Calls You

Fulton, Missouri: 1998 - Denver, Colorado: 2001

Late in undergrad, well known for my love of dance (even when sober), I wanted to apply for a graduate degree in dance therapy, imagining I could actually have a job where I helped people and moved all day. I simultaneously wondered at the age of twenty-one—*How am I going to get paid for that?* Dance therapy was a salable skill in big cities in the seventies and eighties, working in hospitals with the inpatient in groups, but I was in the wrong decade for job hunting with that type of degree. In some sense, I was right and wrong. As a result, I rerouted my career pursuit to industrial/organizational psychology, yet another degree that left me spending a decade attempting to perfect my elevator pitch explaining my exact skill set. When people would ask, "What do you do?" and I responded with, "industrial/organizational psychology," 100 percent of the time, it was followed up with, "Now what is that?"

I thought I/O psychology would equate to a stable, high income with engaging work, but what I failed to consider was my emotional self, the part of me that desired a calling, not just a job. Again, my head drove the bus while my heart took the backseat. I believe some of us have callings, and some of us prefer to work a job; neither is right or wrong, just different. A calling comes to us in an ache, urging us to keep going in the direction of our passion in a way that pushes us through obstacles others would read as a reason to quit. A calling will move us past all rationale to pursue a dream. It is a blessing and a curse.

This drive will seduce you to spend all your free time on a pursuit, create free time you don't have, lose sleep just for the possibility of an opportunity to make your passion come to life. It is like chasing a single firefly in a pitch-black forest, moving closer to the glow when it lights up, and losing it when it goes dark, slowly moving closer to catching it over time, but with no guarantee that little glow-worm will end up in your palm. Even if it does, you may decide to just let it go anyway. It is that messy. Maybe even an obsession, and for many who have the stamina, the ache that drives you through every setback over the years will result in some success but not always what you imagine. The notion of the overnight success, except for maybe a TikTok-er or two, is really the culmination of small wins year after year until something bigger happens. I have observed this over the years with Mark's art, as well. I think the same grit that is built through pursuing dreams also helps with getting through loss. All the failures along the way are little grief practices that prepare us for the inevitable suffering that comes with life.

Most of my friends had graduate degree plans lined up by second semester senior year, and I did too with my fancy I/O program, but I still wavered a bit. After graduation, my girlfriend and I backpacked across Europe with a Eurail pass, an international calling card (pre cell phones), and some divine intervention. I imagine now how different that adventure might be, not having to carry around an actual guide with phone numbers for hostels, using payphones for booking, and actual maps for public transportation. Cell phones and Google have changed the world, and those started out as someone's dreams once.

An event from our adventure that still cracks me up to this day highlights the effects of growing up with a feeling of safety in the world, which shapes how we evaluate our environment for the rest of our lives. Three of us were traveling from Poland to Prague on an overnight train after splitting up with my friend's brother and another friend so we could detour to visit Auschwitz and meet up with them in a few days. Traveling through the country in the late nineties by coal train in Eastern Europe was eye-opening; we passed many homes where families were clearly gardening for sustenance and did not have running water. The poverty was beyond anything I'd seen in the US, even in our inner cities or rural communities.

There I was, sitting on a train, facing backward, listening to my music, not speaking a lick of Polish except the words repeated to me as a child in a story about my great grandmother's parrot. Legend has it he sang this phrase, phonetically: "Eccch duh domo spach," Which, translated, means "Go home and go to bed" to all who entered the house.

Facing me a few rows away was a man who looked older than my grandfather, wrapped in a gray wool coat too large for his frame. Deep creases decorated his thick skin, the stories of his life etched in the lines of his face. His smiling eyes watched me, and I nervously smiled and looked back out the window. At one of the stops, deep in the country, peering out, I could only see a few simple cottages with outhouses and yards used to grow root vegetables. My silent friend got up to get off. Passing by, his peaceful eyes caught mine, and he handed me a tiny origami crane that I have kept to this day. The crane symbolizes peace, happiness, long life, love, and prosperity, depending on who you ask. He only spoke with his eyes, gifted me his crane blessing, and exited the car. It was the oddest, sweetest gesture from a stranger who appeared to have nothing.

Traveling in places where we don't know anyone or speak the local language, we are forced to rely on the kindness of others to guide us. In many ways, those experiences in my twenties helped shift my view of being safe in the world. Many experts in the trauma field say that trauma robs us of a sense of safety in our bodies and the world. A small act of connection and kindness from this stranger was deeply healing on some level, unlike the next part of our train travels.

After visiting the concentration camp, we hopped on the train bound for Prague overnight. The three of us were in a compartment with two benches facing each other, packs stowed on luggage racks overhead. As the night progressed and the train rattled on down the tracks, we kicked our feet up and tried to get some sleep. Around midnight, the train stopped moving, and we were puzzled, glancing out the window for clues. After what felt like hours, we heard a cacophony of men's voices yelling, shouting, and screaming, running end to end through the aisle of the train car. Unsure of our location, the voices, the language, or the country, my heart began racing. Where the fuck are we?!

I quickly took my belt and looped it through the handle of the door of the train car, creating a makeshift lock for our little cabin. The voices grew louder, incessantly banging on every cabin door as they ran through, rattling door handles, potentially looking for open compartments. The hot washes of fear burned through my veins as I contemplated how strong my little belt may or may not be. Meanwhile, my bestie was sitting next to me, snoring, mostly asleep. I was alert and awake for hours while these men circled through the cars again and again. In the silence, my imagination filled with images of them busting open the door and kidnapping us, or worse. Fed by this toxic adrenaline elixir, I sat awake all night, praying for daylight to return swiftly, like she was some kind of superhero coming to save us.

In between one of their rounds, another crew of men came through banging on the doors— shouting, banging, shouting, banging—until they hit our door. Pounding, urgently telling us to open up, I thought, *But what if this was the group that had been circling all night? What if it was a scam to get us to open our door?*

A quick vote among the three of us, open the door won, so I unbuckled my belt lock. In the dark aisle stood the local military carrying machine guns, accompanied by dogs with muzzles, demanding our passports in some unknown language. Flashlights lit up our dreadful passport photos as they scanned our faces for a match. They handed our passports back, and we relocked our door. This pattern went on all through the night. The rowdy crowd of men would raid the train, the military would sweep the train, and as the train pushed on, the wild group would return only to hide at the next stop during the military sweep. When we finally parked safely the following morning, we exited the train greeted by two rows of soldiers with machine guns and muzzled dogs.

Overcome with relief, the worry sickness melted out of my tired body. When I turned to Morgan and said, "I was up sick all night because I was so scared," she started laughing and said, "Eh, they could have just been happy soccer fans partying it up after a good game." Either story could have been true. We will never know, but had I felt a general sense of safety in the world, I might have just thought they were soccer players, too, or a rowdy harmless party. All of the possibilities would have been available to my imagination, not just the scariest one. I imagine my lack of security in the world stems not just from my own trauma, like almost getting kidnapped, but from our familial trauma.

My father's mother died from cancer when he was four, and I grew up in an extended family that never really moved past her death, along with a mentally ill grandfather. My mother's family also had a history of trauma and mental illness, which, combined with my own life experience, was not a setup for a feeling that "the world is a safe place."

Trauma is actually passed down through our epigenetics. My trauma in my life can impact my genes in a way that is transferred to my children. Trauma affects how we see people, the environment, and the actions of others, because when we have experienced trauma, we become superefficient at detecting potentially similar situations that harmed us in the past. We become hyperaware of details that are similar to the original trauma. The challenge becomes that trauma over-sensitizes us to environmental triggers, and we fail to recognize when we are safe. This over-sensitization creates hypervigilance, where we are constantly attuned to potential threats and can no longer assess the elements that indicate we are actually safe. Like a microscope magnifying one bacteria cell amid one thousand skin cells, what we see is bacteria, but what we are looking at is skin. Trauma is not an event that happens to us; it is our relationship to what happens to us and becomes something we live day in and out in our perceptions of people, our environment, and the stories we tell ourselves, which, I believe, is how grief can become something we never heal from. Not because of the loss, but because of the meaning of the loss—the loss combined with all of our previous experiences and whether we have emotional support after.

My European adventure was fun and scary at times, and by the end, I was ready to return home. I flew back in December 1998 and was supposed to begin graduate school in Colorado in January 1999. After a week or so, with my feet back on US soil, I called the professor who ran the program to tell him I wouldn't attend, even though they had deferred my start date to the spring semester, because I wanted to venture off to Africa instead.

Shortly after that call, sitting in my dad's office, I asked him if I could train as a programmer or go into IT like he and my brother when I finished traveling. He told me I would be bored, to come up with another plan. I cried, and then the next day, called my professor back to say that I was, in fact, going to attend school in January as originally planned.

My dad asked me shortly after, "What are you going to do if you don't like industrial/organizational psychology?"

I said, "Well, I'll just go back to grad school."

I guess "going back to school" was always in my plan, whether I knew it or not. Perhaps, had I not lost access to my intuition for those few years, I would have appreciated the writing on the wall, but alas, I was young, hopeful, and most problems seemed solvable with more education and student loans. Ahhh, the nineties!

I hopped on a plane to Denver with one bag and stayed with a distant family friend while I found an apartment and started my Master's. I fantasized about working in this field; I would help combat inequity in the workplace, thereby creating healthier work environments.

My first job after earning my degree was consulting for a firm that developed selection and promotional testing for police and fire departments. What I found in a couple of brief years was that we were hired to implement valid selection and promotion systems, and because firms used our tools, they had a solid legal defense against adverse impact and

Equal Employment Opportunity lawsuits. I was participating in a system of oppression, and my heart couldn't take it. Really, my role was to prevent these departments from getting sued for discrimination, not much else, which is different than creating an equitable work environment. I wasn't helping reduce instances of oppression or unfair hiring; I was "helping" the old systems that have been in place for years continue to operate in much the same ways, but now with a rock-solid legal defense. Yikes! Poof! My occupational bubble burst. When my department was liquidated in late 2001, post-9/11, it was a blessing in disguise.

Flashback: When I read or hear "9/11" anywhere, I immediately flash to the moment when I found out the towers had been hit, and I can see the TV screen with the surreal images of tower one getting struck, calling my brother in NYC to make sure he was okay, and then the silence in the skies afterward. This is trauma, a trauma trigger, something in the present day that flashes us to a moment in the past that we can either see, hear, taste, smell, sense—sometimes with a connection to a moment in history, sometimes not. Sometimes it is just a feeling without a concrete memory attached.

After getting laid off, I felt hopeless about my future and thought I had wasted my time on that degree. Why did I go to grad school with no work experience? So dumb! The questioning and self-doubt were deafening. Now, I look back and kind of laugh at my idealistic self. I admire her and laugh, because unwanted degrees are a totally solvable problem—more education (cough). What next? I did what anyone in their early twenties might do with an unfolding existential crisis: I moved to Hawaii for six months with a dear friend from college. I had air miles from consulting to buy one ticket, a severance package, and unemployment while I looked for jobs; what could possibly go wrong?

I thought the ocean, sun, and whales would have answers for my soul. I'm not sure what I found on that island of sand and volcanic rock except clarity that I could not go backward and that riding waves gave new meaning to letting go. Riding waves is now used to treat trauma; it forces you into a flow state which is therapeutic. In our culture, we operate in Gamma, Beta, and some Alpha while awake, but our intuition and creativity lie between Alpha and Theta, also known as the flow state. Personally, I believe this is where trauma heals itself. Find your flow, and your body will tell you how to recover. When eight- to ten-foot waves break onshore, you can only get in and out of the ocean when she lets you.

Sometimes I would think, *Ride this one in*, only to not get pushed in far enough and have the undertow pull me back out until the next set. Losing a wave in white water was similar: I would have to relax while the water pushed me down and then surface once the surge passed.

The ocean is much like the emotional body. Feelings have a ride of their own, and we must learn not to try to push to the surface too soon before we are unburied by the feeling. We must hold our breath (totally true that in panic, one should hold their breath initially to balance O2!), stay calm, and rise up when the weight lifts. I had to move forward, and maybe that has always been in me, even before her—the idea that when I don't know my next move, I just make a move, any move, because my response will give me more information. Never stay stuck for too long.

When I found out she had died, I just knew I had to deliver her right away and begin to move; I couldn't sit and wait to be ready. It is like that in running our own businesses, as well; I can't always wait to feel ready or know for sure what my next move will be. I have to dare to be wrong at the risk of something magical.

Don't get me wrong, I am terrified of making mistakes, and sometimes my moves are just wrong, but they bring clarity. Before I taught my first Nia class, I practiced a one-hour routine for six months. Ten years later, I can still lead that routine front to back without any preparation. When a calling calls me, I am always scared, terrified even. I just don't ever let my fear stop me, generally speaking, except maybe jumping out of airplanes! Although even that, I wonder if I might try one day.

Five cycles of the moon in the sand, and the gig was up, money gone, so I traveled back to Colorado and found a job working as an assistant in a high-tech firm. I was way overqualified for the job that I accepted, but I thought just to get my foot in the door and figure out what comes next, and here is where Mark comes in.

Our mutual friend from my first job, who had introduced us on a camping trip a year earlier, took me out to lunch and afterward told Mark I was back in town. I swear I returned to Colorado and called him, but he thinks he heard I was back, and he called me. The devil is in the details, and I'm not sure we will ever know the truth. Somehow, one of us called the other, and we began dating, engaged a year later, married a year after that.

After we married, I decided that I had to give dance therapy a try. I had spent seven years, give or take, in the business world trying to find my way, and I was having headaches and stomach aches, difficulty sleeping, and severe anxiety. It became more and more challenging to get through a day at the office; my body was telling me that I needed something more meaningful, which propelled me back to grad school at Naropa University in Boulder, Colorado for dance therapy. Ah yes, my first whisper of intuition. Had I just listened to that first calling, I would have saved myself a chunk of money.

In my family, we have this joke about how many degrees are in any given room on a holiday, because almost everyone in the family has at least two degrees, if not more, my dad topping out at maybe two Master's and a Ph.D. Education is always the answer, at least so I thought. Education was initially a way to keep women out of a field of occupation. I believe getting degrees now is an attempt to even the playing field, but in reality, as women, our superpowers are not learned in books; they are learned through relationships.

So back at it, in school again, I started to slow down, meditate more, and practice body-based psychotherapy, and this learning was different. It wasn't just about the mind; it was about the body, too. Early in the program, a professor said, "In our culture, the mind rules over the body, but here we say the mind and the body offer equal wisdom." That change in worldview brought some odd experiences that began to make me wonder about how I viewed life.

One night, not being able to sleep, I flicked on the TV. At the time, the TV would occasionally short randomly, but as I was sitting there in the dark, I thought to myself, *This TV is about to flick off, and it is going to freak me out.* Guess what? It did. That little voice in my belly was getting clearer.

Around this same time, I had had this vivid dream about my younger brother, where I was in the grocery store, and someone came up to me to tell me that he had just been in an accident and hit his head at sixty miles an hour. He was a road biker, so I thought maybe it was my anxiety about him road biking windy Colorado roads. I called and told him about the dream and said, "Isn't that weird?" and he said, "Bec, I just bought a motorcycle yesterday" impulsively. Eeeeek! He turned around and sold the bike; at least, he told me he did.

So, I had been down the road of Catholicism, and a priest once called me a "cafeteria-style" Catholic. Through studying anthropology/sociology/psychology, I had become an atheist, but now I was starting to question that. My pendulum had swung in two opposite directions, and I began finding this middle: considering some spirituality, still very skeptical, but unable to deny some of my experiences. Swimming with sea turtles will do that to you.

As for the Catholic part, I think I went through with all of it because my friends were doing it. I knew after my first penance, where I went to "confess" my sins at the age of twelve, that the church wasn't for me. When my turn came to do penance, I was directed to the room in the back that they used to call the "crying room," where caregivers could take their loud children during mass. The visiting priest, whom I had never met, was sitting in a folding chair, hands clasped outside of his robe, and gestured with a nod as I entered. I took my seat face to face with him, about a foot or two apart. Nervous, sweaty, hoping I would remember the order of the ritual, Father began the process, and we got to the part of confessing.

At that age, I didn't really have any notable sins to share, so I did what I thought good Catholic girls do and made some up, right there in the face of god and the priest, in his holy den. Lies that would just get me through this thing, a fib or two about being mean to my brothers. I couldn't lie too much, because then I would have to confess lying in another confession. There seemed to be some happy medium that satisfied me. Apparently, my lies were transparent; the lion began to stalk.

"Have you ever had inappropriate thoughts? Maybe touch yourself inappropriately?"

Thank gdess for that gut feeling; this gazelle was ready to run, my stomach twisted, cheeks on fire.

I demurely responded, "No, Father," and prayed to anyone to get me the fuck out of there.

I sprinted out of confession, crash-landed in a pew for my penance, recited the Hail Marys and Our Fathers assigned by a likely pedophile, and left the church knowing it was broken, but I wasn't.

How come the church couldn't rattle my value but not being able to have kids could? I have wondered that myself. They recently released names of priests protected by the church for inappropriate interactions with kids, and my first priest was on the list. I remember when he got relocated, everyone was so sad; he was adored by our community. I think that was the day my heart broke for the Catholic church. I wasn't there for god but to socialize with my girlfriends; maybe that was the real divine connection. Relationships are the root of healing.

Back in grad school, Mark's part-time job as a programmer was drying up. He had been working part-time for a consulting firm since before we met. He, too, had picked a few careers along the way: started out in school for engineering, decided that wasn't meaningful enough, and graduated with a philosophy degree. Deciding art couldn't pay the bills, post-college, height of the Internet boom, Mark took a programming aptitude test with a big firm and achieved one of the best scores of all candidates. As a result, he was immediately hired and trained to be a web developer in 2000. For a handful of years, he worked full-time as a web developer on different projects. After a phase in his career that he refers to as "sitting the bench" (he was trained, but there was no work, so he got to just hang out at home with a paycheck), he decided to start painting in earnest to pass the time. After about a year of bench sitting, he sold his expensive car, bought the old Jeep, and went back to grad school at CU Boulder for art when we met in 2001.

Standing in the dining room, cheap chandelier overhead, wondering how my part-time income was going to cover the bills as Mark's income dwindled, even more, I said, "I don't think you are going to be a professional artist right now." He just stared speechless for a minute. That single sentence hung in the air, like mustard gas, silencing his breath, popping the fate of his deflating dream.

Until now, we had hoped, but hope and desire were not enough to pay the bills. In most creative endeavors, everyone takes "their cut." Well, in general, in the art world, "the cut" is 30 to 60 percent of sales, give or take. Doing the math, you can begin to see how difficult, if not impossible, it may be to piece together a living on art alone. In fact, it is so implausible that I feel like the artist doesn't choose the career, the art chooses them, and they do it because they cannot not do it.

Mark did not become a professional artist overnight, and we did not have a thriving art business overnight. We have worked at it for years and continue to work at it daily amid the chaos of life. I often tell myself that the real business of being self-employed is managing the fear of the unknown that comes along with it: the fear of running out of money, and the fear of failure. But remember the thing about feeling unsafe in the world? I think working for oneself is easier if there is a general sense of safety, like a sense that things will work out.

Feelings such as hope and love are antidotes to fear, worry, and powerlessness. Fear and powerlessness are the seat of trauma. Hope as a felt sense, in my body, is something of a warm opening around the heart with a slight fluttering in the belly—at least for me. Reconnection to that felt sense has guided me through starting businesses and losing babies at the same time. It all happens simultaneously: grief amid the daily requirements of adult life, maybe caring for family, pursuing a career or three, and all the other things that happen. There is no compartment for the loss, no separate place to work through the pain. Moms having babies, caring for babies, losing babies, wishing for babies all happens during all the other demands of adulthood.

Mark took some full-time IT contract work in Denver doing website development, and art moved to the back burner. He was commuting forty miles each way in his old Jeep CJ, frequently coming home smelling like some combination of oil and exhaust, to then trudge out to the detached garage in our condo complex to work on his next masterpiece. The garage had no heat or insulation, so he ran a few electric heaters and hung florescent lighting loosely chained to the ceiling. I attended school, worked; he worked sixty-plus hours a week, painted each night until bed. On weekends, he would travel into the mountains and paint. Rinse, repeat.

When I reflect on those early days of investing time and energy in a dream that I was certain and not certain would amount to something satisfying, I can feel the fatigue, and yet, those early days were easy compared to the rest. It takes so much energy to hold hope, not just for myself but for other people. Holding hope is a gift in my work, and I often consider myself an ambassador of hope.

I almost picture her, Hope, on a chariot, being driven through the darkness of struggle, carrying her glowing pearls of light that sprinkle their blessing on loss, pain, or wishes. She is a warrior and a dreamer and the light of our humanness. When we disconnect from her, the darkness can swallow any of us whole. I have called upon her as something external to me countless times in my journey, and knowing she is out there to be called upon, not something I have to consistently create on my own, somehow eases the pain. I'm never really alone.

So there we were, two young people getting pulled and called into careers that had no promise of putting food on the table, but we kept going.

6

Make A Move

Burlington, Vermont: 2006

In the spring of 2006, five or six years after my dad was diagnosed with an autoimmune disease with an unknown outcome, he called and said that he had been diagnosed with leukemia. It wasn't severe enough for treatment, but it needed to be monitored. I got off the phone in a panic and felt this intense urge to move home. I had left for college at the age of seventeen and moved further and further west for about ten years, never feeling like any new spot was home. Morbidly, I thought, if my dad only has a few years to live, I want to be closer to him while he is alive. At that stage of my life, if I felt like I needed a change, it happened like a reflexive stop, drop, and roll, asking questions like "How?" later.

After the news and the pull back east, I booked us a trip to Burlington, Vermont to explore it as a potential new place to call home. We arrived in seventy-degree temps (highly unusual) and sunny skies (also highly unusual). My parents, brother, and girlfriend met us for the long weekend, and we toured the town and surrounding area. We explored a bit of the Adirondacks, and I attempted to convince Mark that there were plenty of "mountains" there for him to paint, similar to Colorado, selling Burlington as the "Boulder of the East." Lol! Monkey-covering-eyes emoji!

I'm not sure why, but he agreed that he would be creatively inspired in the Burlington area after our short trip. As an artist, he hadn't truly

My cheeks flushed, my eyes began to tear. I started crying and couldn't stop, so we left the cat in the apartment, and Mark ushered me outside to regroup. Fresh air, some dinner, and an SOS call to Mom and Dad saved the day. It was a Saturday, late August, 2006, and Mark was to begin work on Monday, while I was set to start graduate school number three that week as well.

A beer or two later and some problem-solving, our plan B was to find a local hotel for the night to decide the next steps. You cannot actually problem-solve when you are really upset, sad, mad, afraid. If you get really emotional, your rational brain, the thinking part called the prefrontal cortex, goes offline, and you don't have access to it. It is why you can't rationalize with a toddler having a tantrum, nor can you rationalize with a really drunk person; the prefrontal cortex isn't online. So, when someone has blind rage, that is literally true; the part of the brain processing the rage has taken over, and thinking is not happening. When dealing with distraught people, whether at work or in your personal life, regulation before communication is what I always say! So, we got regulated after the shock of the move and apartment and began using our noggins.

That one available hotel room close to town turned into our home for over a week. We unpacked the cat, some clothes, and a few suitcases of faith. Living out of a hotel we couldn't afford, Mark commuted forty miles each way in the U-Haul full of our possessions, parking it in the insurance company's parking lot. I began graduate school and tirelessly called rent ads. Max kept himself undetected in our room most days. I mailed the keys back to the landlord of our first rental, ate the deposit, and luckily found a condo by week's end, where we ended up living for two years. This second condo was by no means charming, but the floors were even, and it had windows sans holes. The carpets on the second floor had a funny smell, and a black line ringed the seam close to the walls. I thought to myself, *Hey, that's what furniture is for—just cover it all up*. That dingy apartment is where we decided to begin a family.

Our bumpy transition from west to east smoothed out over our first year in Vermont. I attended school full-time and worked at an assistantship, while Mark worked as a web developer full-time at a big insurance company. During my second semester of graduate school, I was sitting in the assistantship office working on a network desktop computer, and for some reason, I had this sensation that the printer hooked up to my computer was going to just start printing, even though no one else was in the office. Just then, it started printing and typed something out. Eeek! I froze! Timidly lifting the newly printed paper, I gently flipped it over to reveal the message: "Hello?" More Eeeeek! It was weird that it printed out something, but stranger to me was that I anticipated it. I was starting to get the sense that I could feel things around me in a way that was just a different way of knowing.

Aside from the daily grind of school and one income, the debt of our unsold Colorado condo weighed on us heavily. We were unable to sell it by the time we left; 2006 was the seeding year for what was to become the 2008 real estate crash, and it was just sitting empty. Before class every Monday for an entire semester, we would go around and check in with the cohort one by one. I would report on the stress of having a condo sitting on the market with no reprieve in sight. One income covered two mortgages while I was acquiring more debt. Month after month of renting and carrying the mortgage, we debated renting it, dropping the price, or taking it off the market and going bankrupt. Finally, after about nine months of our condo on the market, we decided to drop the price significantly and "dump it." The real estate market was flooded with too much inventory, and prices were falling. Fifteen-ish years later, the price on that condo, in particular, has recovered tenfold. Real estate 101: Buy low, sell high. We failed it.

So here was my million-dollar decision number two slipping through my fingers, which I would not realize until much later. In order to sell the condo and go to closing with something in the neighborhood of $10,000 to pay the lovely people to buy our condo, we had to come up with cash. Well, way back before I met Mark, I had gotten a small settlement from a car accident. I decided that I would invest some money in a few stocks and try my hand in the stock market. Guess what I invested in? Apple. Fuck me as I write this. It's like the universe has handed us so many opportunities, and if we would just get out of our own way, it could all be easier.

To help us get rid of the condo, we decided to sell our stocks in 2007, which had already doubled, because it had split shortly after I bought it. No, seriously, I'm throwing up in my mouth about what a dumb financial decision all of this was. That is how we have lived life, though. Money is a tool, not an end in itself; the goal is freedom and autonomy, which money offers but not by itself.

So, for me, the takeaway lesson was: We have made money, we have also lost money many times, and we cannot make money if we are not willing to fail and lose. You cannot pursue a dream without fear of maybe losing it all. It all comes together, like yin and yang. The wins, the losses, love and grief, happiness, and sadness.

The daily journey of working for myself is figuring out how I'm going to make money (love this part) and managing my fear of the unknown (hate it). Our first daughter was ultimately the catalyst for moving Mark and I from employees to self-employed. Through the grief, I was able to embrace the sheer terror of living a life with no guarantees, whether it was not knowing where the next paycheck was coming from to not knowing if I would wake up the next day. Once you embrace that as your truth, there is no stopping you.

7

One Step Forward, One Step Back

Burlington, Vermont: 2007

Once we gave our condo away and were free from that, as well as our future millions in Apple stock (fuck me!), there was more room to pursue gallery representation in Vermont. Mark still had artwork in the Colorado gallery, but we needed to find local representation. Although the art market is international, landscape art is somewhat regional. I did some research and found every gallery in Stowe and Manchester, Vermont that sold representational art and pitched Mark's work to them. At that point, in 2007, Mark's vitae included an award from an Estes Park plein air event and representation at one gallery. Not very impressive. I was selling a dream, a young artist with budding potential, but not much else.

Sometimes there is that one lead, and sometimes that opportunity is a win, and sometimes it is a loss, but sure enough, I heard back from one gallery owner in Stowe out of dozens of emails and phone calls. It was a dribble away from complete rejection, but I figured one interested response was better than none.

Rejection. I've never gotten comfortable with it. I now just accept it as a part of life. It never gets easier, but we have learned to ride the wave of feelings that come with it. The response was from the Green Mountain Fine Art Gallery owner, and she was interested in meeting Mark and seeing his work in person. It only takes one "yes" to make the next right move.

We trekked up to the gallery one Saturday, located on the main road through Stowe, with a carload of poorly framed artwork. She was excited about his work, and it felt like a good fit. She told some horror stories of other local galleries not paying their artists after selling work, so I thought there was no way she would do anything like that, which seemed like the most significant risk in entering new galleries. Sometimes galleries go under and take off with all the commissions. So, we signed an agreement for representation, and she planned to do some marketing for Mark's work and put him in a show in the summer and fall. The shows would give us a feel for how his work might be received in the market. Like most things, art is a bit of a gamble, and it can be tough to predict how successful an artist's work will become. A lot of skill, the right relationships, and a bit 'o magic gives art its wings.

Concurrently, I began researching plein air events which were popping up all over the country; it was a reemerging trend in representational work. These events select artist participants by either jury or invitation. For juried shows, an accomplished artist or panel of artists reviews submissions from prospective artists who would like to compete in the event, and a juror(s) selects the artists who will participate. Other plein air events might be "invitationals," and artists are simply invited by the organizing body to participate based on their experience, notoriety, subject matter, and/or skill. Once selected for an event, artists will all visit a specified location over the course of a few days or weeks to paint outside on location. At the end of the event, the paintings are hung wet, judged, and sold to collectors. Awards from these events tend to carry some weight in helping establish the artist's reputation, and usually come with decent cash prizes, too. At the end of a week, some artists submit anywhere from one to ten paintings—all done quickly, outside, from life.

Mark's specialty has always been plein air work; he adventures outside year-round, no matter what the temperature, and paints from life.

In fact, even if he paints a studio piece, he starts by painting a study outdoors. After a few years of being with him and around his art, I could tell the difference between paintings created in a studio or from life. I have always described it as the "spirit" of the painting. When done from life, a piece of work has a spirit that resonates deeply with people, and when painted from a photo, it does not, and you can feel the difference. Many great artists have encouraged young students to go and paint from life as much as possible, whether landscape or figure, for this reason.

Along with pitching galleries, I strongly encouraged Mark to apply for Plein Air Easton , one of the most significant plein air events in the country at the time. He did, and surprisingly, he got in. This all felt like big time; he was in a gallery in Stowe and got into one of the biggest plein air painting events in the country. Success felt so close, but it would be years and years of these kinds of wins before he launched a full-time career.

Summer bloomed, and we traveled to Easton together and experienced the thrill and stress of a big, top tier, plein air event for the first time. It was all new to us, and most spouses did not tag along, but I wanted to see what it was all about. Mark painted a landscape each day, and evenings we attended scheduled events to meet other artists and collectors. There was a club of artists who traveled the country doing these types of events, and Mark was young and new, not part of the group. Quickly, we started learning it is much like any business: Who you know really matters. Sometimes, in these situations, knowing less is actually more helpful. If I knew then what I know now, I probably never would have pitched Mark for that show, just like the first art fair. He had skill, but he was one artist among so much renowned talent—artists well known and collected in the region. No matter what the game, it is tough to compete with local favorites. Lesson number 501: Know your audience.

The competition and stress are challenging. Bigger is better, and early on, Mark painted small works, roughly 8x10 to 18x24. He painted some pretty scenes during the week, but he was really drawn to paint an old slave cabin out on some property one day. The cabin was dark, built with weathered wood, one room with a brick floor. As usual, I was hanging out, mucking around, meditating, checking things out while Mark was painting the entrance. I was walking around mindfully when I kept getting these chills up my back in a particular spot in the cabin. It was inky, unlit with few windows, also somewhat eerie. As I was exploring this empty room, I was drawn to a spot on the floor to the right of the door toward the front of the structure. I kept getting this hit that there was something buried under these few bricks in the floor. My curiosity and perhaps boredom was getting the best of me, so I leaned down and touched one of the bricks, wanting to see what else might declare itself.

I got this idea that I could move the brick, so I gently pulled on an edge to see if it would lift, and it quickly shifted up. I tugged a little more and slid the brick out. It was totally loose and just resting in the sandy earth, but there was no way for me to know that before removing it from the floor. I thought, *Holy shit,* and then wondered if it was just one brick or more. I gawked at the sandy bottom and reached over to the next brick. It slid out as well. I freaked out, fearing I might unearth a body, so I quickly returned the bricks back to their sandy nests and ran out. I told Mark, and he laughed at me. Ah, so typical. Who knows what is buried there? I will never know. Perhaps nothing, but my intuition scared me. My intuition has served me so much in my healing that now it doesn't scare me like it did back then; it has just become part of a way of knowing the world. My voice of intuition is quiet and grounded, not alarming; very matter-of-fact, disconnected from the outcome or emotion.

Mark finished up his painting, and we brought it back to the pool house where we were staying. It was the last evening before judging, and we lined up his paintings on the floor, admiring them. We were joking about one of them being an "award winner." But, seriously, none of them, no offense to Mark and his talent, were award winners. They were shimmering with promise but not in the same league as the other artists.

The next evening, all dressed up, excited to see all the work and meet some artists, we headed to the venue. Each artist picked two pieces for judging that hung on the wall to begin the show, and Mark had entered *Slave Cabin* and a painting of an artist painting a sailboat, both reasonably small works. When we arrived, we strolled around the rooms hung with all the artists submissions from a week of painting, looking at the display of enormous paintings with bright colors, and excitement fizzled to dread. Mark's work was small and somewhat forgettable compared to the other submissions. We left after circling the collection once.

Mark was so upset. He says to this day, "I got my ass kicked." He sold one painting to the owner of the pool house where we were staying, because he painted her sailboat. It was a defining moment in Mark's career. He had had some success selling work, but when compared to the top plein air artists in the country, he was barely at the bottom in terms of skill and talent, so much so that he did not get into the show the following year. He was in a total funk, and I thought he might just throw in the towel and burn the brushes right then, never to return to painting.

Ah well, but if anyone knows an artist, you know that the moment they feel discouraged or challenged is the exact moment that they turn back toward the canvas with intensified rigor and resolve. As therapists, we may or may not refer to that as trauma bonding, but in school, they always taught me not to therapize my partner, so I'll just leave that there.

Maybe like life, having children, careers, birthing just about anything, with every move forward, there is a push backward. I always say to clients that growth is not linear, success and progress are not linear. Progress and process looks more like a loop-dee-loop roller coaster with a slight incline, filled with moments of grief, defeat, thrill, terror, and joy. It is the journey as much as the outcome that becomes the motivation and fulfillment. In this way, there is always a new peak to set as a new goal; it never really stops.

Easton was disheartening, but Mark was having some success in the Stowe gallery, so where one door slammed shut, another opened. Selling paintings through the gallery helped build confidence that we could create a New England market for Mark's work, because until then, he had only sold work out west.

That summer, he came back and tackled greens with new enthusiasm, plugged away, and the dream seemed more impossible than ever, like chasing the bottom of a rainbow after a storm. As he dove into becoming a better artist, I explored ways to have an art business. From early on, I knew that the only way for this whole thing to work was to sell and market Mark's art on our own, at least in part, but I had no idea how to do that.

8

Healing Is A Practice

Boulder, Colorado: 2002

Injuries happen, accidents happen; healing doesn't just happen all the time. Healing requires practice, just like learning a sport or skill. I often say the day I can't heal something with dancing, a walk, breathing, or a hot bath might be my last day of living.

Growing up, I played soccer with the boys, because there were no girls teams. I ice-skated, skied, danced, had a stint with softball, basketball, and golf, eventually played soccer in college. Movement was a part of my childhood as much as annoying chores and hours spent twisting the spiral phone cord around my fingers as many times as possible while chatting on the phone with friends. When I was younger and in a mood, my mom would tell me to go run. Even though I don't think I ever liked running, it helped shift my mindset.

Fitness has always been a part of my life and part of the driver for moving to Colorado in the first place. I saw that rec path through downtown Denver while visiting on a college ski trip and thought, *I could get used to this!* As most things go, I don't think I ever used that path, even when I lived there, except to trek out to a nightclub or two, go figure. Nonetheless, while living in Colorado in my twenties, running was my default workout when not hiking, biking, or skiing.

In the summer of 2002, I was headed home with a friend from a James Brown concert (yes, he was fantastic in concert and wore a wild, blue, shimmery suit) on that two-lane highway out of Steamboat Springs. Cruising along, laughing about the weekend shenanigans, Matt, my friend driving, suddenly noticed that we were rapidly approaching a cyclist on the right side of the shoulderless road. In a moment of panic, he began to swerve into oncoming traffic to avoid the cyclist, where we were faced with an eighteen-wheeler barreling toward us. He quickly corrected and plowed on the brakes. Burning rubber and fishtailing, we skidded to a stop. In the slice of a second, we avoided the cyclist, and BAM! My eardrums vibrated with the sound of smashing cars at high speed, broken glass sprayed through the vehicle, the smell of crunched metal and hot rubber singed my nostrils. Time hiccupped. In the illusion of a pause, I realized that we had been hit. I checked myself for blood, pain, and ability to breathe. All clear.

I look at Matt. No blood, he's talking, but everything is coming to me through this funnel of consciousness, muted and cloudy. I crack open the car door and slide out of my seat, and it rebounds like a slinky. The head of the seat lurches toward the front windshield where it stays, no longer bolted down to the car. I'm standing now, no pain, no broken bones. I'm okay. The rear bolts had been ripped out from the impact, and only the front bolts remained anchored. Taking in the scene, I see the car is now half the size it was a minute ago, and a full-size SUV grill is inches from the backs of our seats, rammed through the back end of this small VW Golf.

I walk to the roadside and am oddly coherent; I can see everyone is walking around, and I just sit in the tall grass noticing no one is visibly injured. I take a few breaths and talk to myself out loud to bring myself back into my body, whispering, "You made it, you are safe, you are okay, breathe."

The one cop from a neighboring town shows up, sees our car, and says, "You were lucky you weren't scalped and didn't go through the windshield; I've seen that so many times in my career." Then he takes some notes and tells the car full of kids behind us that they need to be transported to the hospital via the ambulance on scene because they are minors. If I want to go via ambulance, I must wait until it comes back to the scene to pick me up, maybe an hour. I pass and hitch a ride with friends back to Boulder to the ER where they tell me I just have soft tissue damage and I'll be fine. My seat became detached from the base of the car, and I walked away. There was a little bit of magic that day, a big blessing. That moment could have changed the direction of my life like so many others.

When we are still living, our success rate for survival is 100 percent; we have survived 100 percent of our darkest hours. I can still smell that crash, though: bent metal, burnt rubber, and broken glass. Who knew that had a smell? But it does, and if I smell any of those things to this day, I am spun into that moment right after impact, sitting in the car, where time stopped, and my brain was trying to catch up with what my body had just endured. That is trauma, a sensory experience, like a smell, sound, taste, scent. Hearing a song will bring a moment from the past to the present, and our body responds to that moment brought forth. Trauma does not know time; it ellipses her.

Luckily for me, I am aware that now if my heart starts racing in the present moment when smelling tangled metal, it is not about what is happening in the present moment but the past. My heart racing is actually in response to the car accident years ago, not the smell I am smelling now, and I can consciously put that reaction back in the past with that memory of the car wreck where it belongs.

What happens, though, if I have that somatic memory? I smell metal, my body tenses, my heart races, but I don't have the mental flash of the car accident? Or the bus driver? Or the priest? How would I know that the response in my body was related to the past and not the present moment? I wouldn't—that is also trauma. The body remembers what the mind doesn't, and when it responds to the past without a solid memory in our mind's eye, we experience it as the present and attempt to make sense of it in the moment. Trauma is a ghost that haunts unless we put it back to rest in the past, again and again. That is the practice, putting the ghostly memories back in the past and not allowing them to take up residence in the present. Grief and loss are trauma, and that is life for all of us.

I walked away without a scratch, but I had chronic back and neck pain for a few years after that accident. Running, the practice that kept me sane, became more and more challenging. Old habits die hard, and unable to accept that my body needed something else, I continued pushing. Just push through, just push through. A year later, I trained and ran a half marathon. Afterward, my knees ached so badly, along with my whole body, so much so that I could hardly walk. Upon finishing, I wondered, *Why am I doing this? Am I running away from something or towards something?*

Around the same time, I was working next door to a Nia fitness studio in Boulder and decided to try it out during lunch hour one afternoon. I took Jill's class, and I loved it. She was my first instructor, and I was one of her early students. After the first few classes, I was hooked; I found that I could work out and experience joy simultaneously. It combines dance, martial arts, and the healing arts done in the bare feet, focusing on moving the body in ways that feel joyful and nourishing. We shouted "YES" a lot while moving. It may sound funny, but when you shout "yes" with your mind, body, spirit, it creates an incredible, uncrushable power, kind of like hope.

I couldn't believe it—a fitness practice that felt good! What? No pain, no gain? While running, I realized I spent most of my time trying to find ways to avoid paying attention to what I was doing by listening to music, watching the scenery, planning—whatever I could do to keep my awareness out of my body, because my body hurt while running. I found in Nia I could get fit and maintain attention to sensation in my body, because I wasn't pushing to the point of pain and exhaustion. I could move for the simple joy and pleasure of moving. I felt Joy, a radiating warmth from my heart and belly, and there was no thinking.

There are two neural pathways to pleasure in the body, joy/excitement or relief from pain. I think of the first as an adrenaline rush and the second as more of an opiate rush, all the natural drugs created in the body. Get high on your own supply! After many years of using movement to heal from physical injuries to emotional trauma, grief and loss, my theory is that even the weight loss market that focuses on calories alone is failing, because really joy creates sustainable practices that help the body burn energy more efficiently.

There is a high correlation between female obesity and childhood trauma. When we feel better, we heal more efficiently and lose weight and get stronger more effectively. The physical and emotional body are one thing, they are not separate, and when we try to address an issue in the physical realm without addressing the emotional realm, we are less successful. When we take things like joy and relationships out of fitness, just like we have out of medicine, we have taken out the most essential component of our humanness. Any goal we have—weight loss, becoming a professional artist, healing from grief—all require access to joy and relationships.

If hope can predict outcomes in the effects of HIV on the body, so can hope affect our ability to lose weight. In fact, studies show that imagining the activity we are doing is beneficial for our health improves the effectiveness of that activity. So, if I imagine housework is helping my blood pressure, it actually does help my blood pressure more than if I didn't have that intention. The same is true of weight loss; belief is a powerful tool.

Joy is a practice like healing I choose fitness and movement that brings me joy because joy doesn't just happen. But the more time I spend practicing joy, the easier it is to experience. Joy and love are the two regulating emotions for feelings like fear, loneliness, sadness, grief, anger, shame, guilt, etc. We get regulated by intentionally moving ourselves from our pain into a more peaceful pleasure state; it is a practice and does not happen quickly all the time. Emotional movement is tied to physical movement, which is essential in healing.

As humans, we are actually hardwired to notice scary and/or threatening things and changes in our environment—elements that may be associated with negative emotions. We are also better at remembering the circumstances in which difficult things have happened in our lives and the details around those events. This allows us to better detect challenges and threats in the future. We are highly effective threat detectives!

In a way, being human, we are hardwired for negativity. Practicing joy, love, and peace does shift our neurobiology over time, but it is a practice; we don't do this naturally. We can work on accessing those feelings through sensation; feelings are sensations in the body, just like memories.

When we decided to relocate from Boulder to Burlington in 2006, I researched Nia instructors in the area, and there were none teaching regularly. Like most things, if there is something that I want and it does not exist, I create it. I decided to do the first level of Nia training, the White Belt, in the spring of 2006, right before our big move east, to start a Nia community in Vermont. After the training in March, I spent six months teaching myself how to conduct a Nia class, because I felt like I could not live without this practice in my life. Six months to learn fifty minutes of choreography, and I never got bored; I found it fun.

In preparation, I taught a class to my mom in her living room, and had only one routine prepared before I began pitching Nia to local gyms in Burlington. I called the local YMCA, introduced myself to the director of fitness, brought in an informational packet, and demonstrated a song or two. The director loved it and agreed to put one Nia class on her group fitness schedule. I was given the small studio on the bottom floor of the Y that had mirrors and a polished stone floor, big enough to fit about six students comfortably. Sometimes I taught classes to one person, and sometimes no one showed up, but I kept showing up, and I kept teaching. That is practice—the discipline to keep showing up, get back on the wagon, start again and again until you can't anymore—and that is the same with healing from pain and injury. I think that is resilience; building resilience and grit is a practice, the getting up and trying again practice, even when feeling defeated.

Showing up to teach repeatedly when just a few people would attend was grueling. It required a certain amount of energy to maintain my enthusiasm. I taught at the Y for about a year around my grad school and internship schedule and grew the confidence to pitch Nia in a few more places. Around the same time, Sabrina, who worked at a local yoga studio and had taken Nia out west, came to the Y to take my classes. After a few of my classes, she convinced her bosses to let me teach a Nia class at 8 a.m. on Saturday mornings in a small studio with cork floors. I mention the surface because, ideally, I would dance barefoot on sprung floors or rubberized floors, so those early years I took whatever I could get. Stone, cork—I would have moved on water if you asked me to.

I again started teaching this early morning class in a small dark classroom in this new location. We began to get a following, and eventually, Sabrina convinced the owners to let me teach this one class in the big studio. They made a little room for me. For about a year, my classes expanded from two to three to twenty-plus students, and the community that grew from that space was a gift. The yoga studio eventually gave me another evening time slot. Then two more Nia instructors moved in from out of town, but we all found one another, and our little Nia community was started and still dances today, over a decade later. It only took a few years and four to five studio pitches, not too bad.

When we dance/move with one another, we see each other's souls in a way. I think other cultures knew this well before we did. Movement for the joy or pleasure of moving is highly regulating for the nervous system, and to move in such a way requires us to be in a balanced and aware state. For example, we can't be afraid and feel the pleasure of articulating the ankle bone; they are competing parts of the nervous system that can't be active simultaneously.

One of my most memorable students was a woman who founded a nonprofit during her stage IV metastasized breast cancer journey. She had neurological symptoms and tumors in her bones that would cause them to crack, but she danced with me in almost every class that I taught. She was my teacher in many ways. In this kind of fitness, I can approach it from any level, and she taught me that the spirit can still dance even when the body can't, which later would become my saving grace after losing a baby.

Movement, any kind, even just the movement of the breath through the nose, helps us cope and heal. Alternating nostril breathing, commonly used in yoga, has been shown to activate the calming part of the nervous system. Healing from grief is about movement. Managing fear is about movement. Statistics show that people who face terrifying situations and can mobilize—fight or flight—suffer far less from PTSD than those who freeze or faint. We have no control over how our body unconsciously responds, and there is no guarantee we will react the same way twice.

With the growing Nia community, my friend had aspirations for her own studio. I did not, so it was a fantastic opportunity to dive in together to create a space. In the fall of 2008, Sabrina opened her studio, and I taught free Nia classes that week. We had a packed house, thirty-plus in a class, and that was when the home of Nia was founded in our community. I still, to this day, dance with some of the women who danced with me on the stone floor in the Y over ten years ago now. These women have danced with me through the deepest sorrows of my life and the most remarkable accomplishments. It is a little star cluster of spirits beyond fitness, and I am so glad that I have had the opportunity to be part of it.

Because of this community, I was held in a well of women's tears when our daughter died. Community is essential for healing. We don't do it alone, we aren't meant to; we need each other, we need our people.

In my third pregnancy, I danced until thirty-three weeks, the Wednesday before discovering our daughter had died. These women knew my daughter as well as I did, really, and I feel like that community helped carry me through the darkest hours. After SJ was born, I waited six weeks, and then I got up and danced again and kept dancing. Grief, sadness, depression, anxiety, rage—I danced through it all.

One of the critical things about healing grief is that we each find our own way through the dark valley. Loss, tragic loss, leaves us feeling so powerless. The desire for something to be different, but it can't be; the desire to want it to change, but it won't—that is powerlessness. In grief, we are totally powerless over the loss or change, so an essential part of the healing is having power over our choices around recovery. Having someone tell us what to do to feel better robs us of our ability to move toward our own healing through our own way and perpetuates the powerlessness that was triggered by the loss. In grief, you must find your own way to heal. If you don't, I believe we can get stuck in the trauma of the loss, with no movement around the grief or layers of grief. The trauma can get stuck in the body. Movement, our own chosen movement, is essential.

9

First And Second "Mis"

Burlington, Vermont: 2007

Eager to begin a family, figuring the end of grad school was a good time, we got pregnant in the first month of trying. I thought to myself, *Who knew this would be so easy?* and it made me confident that everything would go as planned.

It was early November. Elated, I told Mark, and we immediately told our family. I scheduled an initial doctor visit and ultrasound and went along my merry way. About six weeks in, before our first ultrasound visit, I started having symptoms indicating a miscarriage. I called the doctor, and she said most likely I would miscarry in twenty-four to forty-eight hours and gave me the "talk" on how common it is, yada yada, as if she had already recited these reassuring statistics ten times today, somewhat cold and matter of fact. I cried, and as quickly as I had adjusted to expecting a child, like a slingshot, I rebounded to the unexpecting mother. I miscarried later that day, and the doctor said we should just try again after a month or so, so we did.

We got pregnant again a few months later in May ('08), no big deal; everything seemed to be working. This part of the journey, the getting pregnant part, can be hugely stressful, but here we were again with the little plus sign on the pregnancy test without much effort. We began our parental journey once again, and I moved back into the planning of an expecting mom. Even though we had a very early miscarriage, and it was sad, I felt like I just moved on with life, busy finishing grad school, internship, working, and teaching Nia. The doctor had said to try again, and I had faith that doing so would bring us home a baby, but little did I know that trying again would turn into seven trying agains.

Around the same time, a dear friend in grad school also announced that she was expecting. We were on a similar timeline with our pregnancies, and it was nice to have a buddy. She and I would attend internship classes together, eat snacks, and swap stories. Everything seemed to be going smoothly. We set up our first ultrasound appointment around six weeks again and anxiously waited for that visit to confirm a growing baby. Until that point, no one really knows what is growing. We can have a pregnancy that never gains a heartbeat, or it just doesn't work out, so, until that first ultrasound, it is difficult to really know anything.

Days ticked on slowly but surely, and I generally felt sick and fatigued all the time. My sense of time during this pregnancy began to slow, as did my ability to go about my daily routine. I remember these weeks where my body felt like it was moving through quicksand just to get through, and the only things I wanted to eat were watermelon and lemonade.

At around six weeks, I went in for an ultrasound with Mark, and there was a little heartbeat. We are just a neural tube, to begin with, our digestive tract with a heart in the middle. So, when we talk about a gut feeling or heart aching, it is actually the first way that we experience the world in our development, just a belly and a heart to start. I've always thought that is a cool way to think about our physical-emotional development.

That little baby was just a bean, and I did not feel very connected to this little being because of our first loss, but we were happy. Le sigh. The repetitive reassurance from doctors and mom-to-be blogs regarding miscarriages all say similar things like, "You know, 75 percent of miscarriages occur before there is even a heartbeat" or something like that. In growing baby land, the first heartbeat seen on ultrasound is the first significant milestone and is typically a good indication the pregnancy is healthy. Ah, yes, we are confident once again, we are in the clear, and I continue as an expecting momma with my plans, dreams, fears, and excitement of what it will be like to have a baby.

The little nugget was measuring appropriately. The heartbeat was strong and had the correct beats per minute (BPMs). Everything looked fine, as fine as anything can look at that stage of development. The ultrasound screen showed us a bean with a bit of flutter in it, indicating the heart, and after a few minutes, they printed some photos and sent us on our way to go and—you guessed it—wait some more.

The black-and-white images of the ultrasound are such a weird thing, really. I still find them floating around my house years later in random stacks of papers. Like what do you do with them? I can't ever throw them away; it feels like I am throwing my kids away. But then when they find their way out of hiding and into the present moment, I am reminded of my losses again. Once you have them, throwing them away seems like a bad omen and somehow makes me a bad mom before I even have a living, breathing child. Like who throws out their own child's baby pictures? But they are not, really; they are like black, white, and gray blobs on bad photo paper with a date on them, showing images that would require special training to decode any time in the future. What they actually are and what they feel like they are are not the same thing. Much like my thoughts, my feelings and behaviors are not the same things. I often say, wanting to do something and doing it are not the same thing . . . maybe that's the key to grit. Doing it versus wanting to do it and knowing the difference.

That spring, I was finishing grad school, which meant taking classes, completing an internship, working as a professor's assistant, growing a tiny human, teaching Nia, buying a house while Mark was working full-time in his web development job, painting full-time whenever he had a free moment. Somehow, that call and connection with the art gallery that I made in Stowe blossomed into a summer show, including Mark's work and several other artists. The show was a success, but mostly I remember sitting outside on a bench because I was so tired. Because I was in my first trimester and had an early loss, I was more reserved about sharing my news with anyone outside the family. At the time, I felt like the gallery owner was totally disappointed in my inability to help sell Mark at the show, but maybe that was more about my own feelings than hers.

Summer seemed busy and slow simultaneously, so much to do with our work, and every day meant one less day of waiting for the next ultrasound. In early August, I began to have some spotting. The reassuring comments from mommas that I knew and the doctors went like this: "Spotting is so common in pregnancy and usually no big deal" or "It is usually just the cervix and has nothing to do with the baby" or "Oh, I had my period every month during all my pregnancies." So, with all that consolation, I felt like this just must be how my body does pregnancy. And almost all miscarriages happen by six weeks, so I must be okay. I convinced myself that I had made it through the riskiest part of the pregnancy in terms of miscarriage, but because I had had a loss already, I went in for an ultrasound anyway.

The ultrasound showed that the little peanut was growing on target, had a strong heartbeat, and they couldn't see any source of bleeding. It all looked normal. I left feeling relieved that the baby was developing well and that the bleeding must be a fluke, so I went home to wait. Everyone had been right; no big deal, just a random symptom and part of normal pregnancy.

The time in between ultrasounds can be like the last half hour of a really long car trip, but instead of it being a solid half hour, that feeling lasts for weeks. Every morning, I would wake up and psych myself up to get through the day, and at the end, I would breathe a sigh that I made it through another twenty-four hours without incident.

But then, one morning, around ten weeks, I woke up and was bleeding more heavily. This seemed more serious. I called the nurse sobbing, and she asked me about my symptoms.

"Are you passing heavy tissue?"

My answer was "No," so she reassured me that everything could be fine. I just needed to come in for a check.

To this day, I wonder if anyone just floats through pregnancy with no fear, no scares, no odd symptoms, no concerns; I'm not even sure that is possible. And really, what else can be done? Worry is not helpful while pregnant, and until any of my pregnancies ended, I was encouraged to hope, hope, hope, and believe that this time we would be rewarded with a healthy baby. Is worry ever helpful? It is some odd way of the brain attempting to control the situation, like if I anticipate all the challenges, and they happen as expected, they won't hurt so bad. But this just isn't true. The tough stuff still hurts, even when we have "prepared" ourselves through the security blanket of worry. So, when I think about a concern, like, *What if this baby doesn't make it?* I consider, *What is the underlying feeling?* For me, it is fear, as well as fear of grief, and then I let myself be scared until I don't feel scared in that moment.

That nurse on that day, though, I did not believe. I had a feeling that things were not fine, that this would be the end of the journey for now with this little babe. He/she was no longer with me. We cleared our morning schedule to go in for the ultrasound. We were escorted into the ultrasound room, and it was the usual routine of hold-my-breath-until-they-tell-me-everything-is-okay. Or not. The doctor inserted the wand, and immediately, an indecipherable monotone gray image appeared on the screen. But what was clear was there was no movement.

She quickly apologized: "I'm sorry, there is no heartbeat."

Quiet tears flowed in gentle streams, the kind that run but have no noise, no crying, because I already knew that was the result. My gut and heart already knew. I was just there for confirmation.

Because I was ten weeks, but the baby only measured eight weeks, or so, I had options. Is that a good thing? I still don't know. Choice A was getting a D&C while knocked out. Choice B: waiting for something to happen naturally. Or Choice C: speeding things up by taking some medication at home to instigate a miscarriage. Being a minimalist when it comes to interventions, I went with Choice C. I rarely take antibiotics and most often will choose the path of most minor treatment possible. I mean, when I was a kid, I would have the dentist do fillings without Novocain! Yikes! Medication affects most people differently, but I am sensitive to most anything—substances, life, emotions, you name it.

So, the "at-home" procedure was more like giving birth than I had anticipated, minus all the excellent drugs, like the ones that would have made me unconscious. Note to self: Don't ever try that at home again. In the evening, I had to insert medication—yes, it is a suppository, and yes, it sucks. It was adding insult to injury, but it was helping me avoid having to go to an operating room and be put under anesthesia for a procedure that had risks of scarring, although rare.

Trauma is about an overwhelming emotional experience getting stuck in the body, something like winding up to swing a bat as hard as possible, but midway through a full-effort strike, you stop the swing abruptly. The wound-up force and energy are all still in the body; it doesn't get a chance to move to completion. That partial swing gets stored as a sensation memory in the body, potentially disconnected from the narrative or the story of the memory. So, for instance, if I imagine the smell of chocolate-chip cookies baking, that is a somatic, emotional memory. I can feel the smell of chocolate-chip cookies baking, and I can feel it in my body without it being attached to a specific cognitive memory—a specific time when I baked cookies.

Somatic memory can have a wide range of presentations, from the yummy smell of baking cookies to the smell of metal crunching from a severe car accident. I use smell as an example, but it can also just be a sensation memory of any kind. It becomes unresolved trauma when the energy of the swing needs to be finished but hasn't, and the feeling awakened in the body is so uncomfortable it is intolerable. This sensation from the past gets relived in the present moment by a trigger: a situation, person, event, smell that reminds us of the experience from the past.

Like a snowball cascading downhill, every time this sensation gets awakened and not resolved, new elements from our experience start to become associated with the overwhelming feelings. So, what began as a sensation from a memory of a car accident now means full-blown panic when I just see a car. Our mind attempts to make sense out of our feelings in the present moment, thus associating them with whatever is happening. So, what once was a memory of an event becomes a sensation we may live out every day, because of all of the triggers that are now associated with it. Trauma is genuinely a haunting of the past surging into the present through sensation, and healing requires identifying triggers and disconnecting those sensations from them, putting the sensation back in the past where it belongs.

Planning to miscarry at home was as much a decision to stay conscious through the whole experience as much as anything, in an attempt to experience it with my physical and emotional body together, so I wouldn't be traumatized by it. Attempting to avoid the ghost of grief, I felt that if I "went under" for the procedure, that the grief would get stuck in my somatic memory, and that it might make it more challenging to move forward with any future pregnancies. I wanted to be conscious through it to feel the pain, all of it, and let this baby go—no truncated swings.

The medication usually kicks in after three to six hours, but of course, my body would do this her own way, and about a half hour after I started the "procedure," I started having intense contractions. Prescriptions that create contractions are not as wise or forgiving as a woman's body; they are irregular, sporadic, and intense from the first one. They don't begin small and get stronger like normal labor. Because they are chemically induced, they start right away at max intensity, are somewhat disorganized, and last for hours. Natural childbirth is like riding a wave of intensity and then relaxation in preparation for the next contraction, but these contractions were intense, on/off, with no predictability, no rhythm. The medication also forces everything to contract, not just the uterus, so I had spasms in all places within the pelvis that one just never wants to have cramps.

I was terribly sick—lying, kneeling, swaying, and humming my way through the pain. I took the pain medication, but it was too late, because I was already in pain, and it was not enough. At least, that was my story. I mean, maybe pain killers don't really work—that's also possible. So, from 3 to 10 p.m., I worked through this pain, terrified of what the end might look like. Humming, humming, and more sounding. For some reason, sounding eased my pain. All these questions were going through my head: *What did I get myself into? What if I hemorrhage and have to go to the ER? Was this the dumbest decision ever? Is this what labor feels like? If so, knock me the fuck out! Oh god, I hope I know when the end of this is near so I am in the bathroom, because I don't want to have to see anything!* On, and on, and on, my mind chatter was so bad, it probably made the Mad Hatter look depressive.

The end finally came. I ran to the bathroom and almost puked in the shower as my body let go of this pregnancy. I went back to bed and went to sleep. I passed out from the relief from pain. I once passed a kidney stone with no drugs, and this was by far more painful, even with medication.

The next day the sun rose. Just like that, I went from being pregnant to not pregnant at all, again. My body started rapidly changing back to prepregnancy. It is truly amazing what the human body can do. I once watched this documentary on how the Catholic church disempowers women by owning the procreation process. By having a life of the soul begin at baptism, the men strip women of the power of creating life and the fact that creating life is one of the most powerful things we do as humans. I found this fascinating and wondered what happened as a woman when I couldn't create life. Who would I become in our society if not a mom? Not because I chose not to have kids, but because maybe I was not able to have kids. I had never spent much of my youth imagining being married or having children. Yet, the idea that I couldn't be a biological mom was becoming a reality, and it was striking at the core of some unknown identity that I didn't even realize I had.

I was grieving, sad and mad that I had spent ten weeks feeding pregnancy hunger. Continuously sick and tired for nothing. I wondered if there was something I could have done, like stopping teaching Nia sooner or stopping working out sooner, that would have helped the process. The doctor said that we could "save the tissue" and have it tested for chromosomal abnormalities, but let's be honest, who wants to do that? I didn't. What was the point?

They said, statistically, it was likely a chromosomal abnormality, and in order to have insurance cover any sort of fertility testing, I would have to have three documented miscarriages in a row, because, evidence suggests that unless you have three in a row, the probability that you have any fertility issues is low. Why isn't this part of the story that we tell our kids? When you start trying to have kids, there may or may not be some early losses, and grief is part of the process. It is all of it—happy/sad, mad/glad, joy/grief . . . you get it all.

In having babies, I learned that statistics are the language of the doctors; they love to hand out statistics regarding every scenario, like salespeople offering schwag at a trade show. It's like as long as the statistics are in your favor, you are just left to hope that things turn out the way they do a majority of the time, and it reinforces the powerlessness. The reality is, the doctors, the nurses, me, and Mark—we were all mostly powerless and swimming in a sea of uncertainty. Where are my sea turtles at?!

Life is created through the body, but there are so many factors influencing the journey. Do you know what most pregnant women do? We wait. Do you know what most OB doctors do? They watch and wait. That's it, people: watch and wait, the best that western medicine has to offer in creating and birthing children in the twenty-first century. They monitor closely with ultrasounds and blood work, help gather information, and can do nothing to save a baby until about twenty-three-plus weeks—and that is the lower limit. Survival rate improves to about 80 percent at twenty-eight weeks of gestation (https://pmc.ncbi.nlm.nih.gov/articles/PMC1117667/).

Finishing up grad school, I buried myself in my work at a local mental health agency on the crisis team. In crisis, we work with clients who are having suicidal or homicidal ideation, decide if clients need to be hospitalized, or meet with clients in the hospital after they have attempted suicide. I have always loved this work. It requires presence and creating plans, and that's it. I've never "taken my work home," so to speak, because I feel like, when I'm working with adults, they are the only ones who control what happens next, not me. I'm a gentle guide for a few hours, no more. But I also don't feel like I'm alone, working in crisis; I am acutely aware that in the grand scheme of life, my suffering is a shared suffering. Everyone who lives experiences some suffering. It is a connector, not a divider.

After the miscarriage, I took some time off, and Mark and I went on vacation. We went to Long Lake with my brother, his wife, and their nine-month-old daughter. It was awesome and sad at the same time. I hiked a mountain and thought I was going to drop over from fatigue. I think it was less than a week after I miscarried—I seriously do not know what I was thinking. I imagine, at the time, I thought I was not going to let anything interfere with our plans and wanted to push through like I had pushed through most things in life.

Summer turned into fall, I went back to working crisis, and started my private practice and teaching Nia. Mark was continuing to work IT at National Life and painting nights and weekends. We agreed that we would take a break and not really worry about family planning for a while.

10

"You Will Have A Daughter...First"

Middletown, Connecticut: 2010

The following spring, sometime in March, visiting my parents in my hometown, my dad asked if it was alright if his shaman came over and did a ceremony for Mark and me. My dad had found Nick through his own healing journey. Many years before, he was diagnosed with stage IV salivary gland cancer, which was rare enough that Sloan Kettering agreed to review a unique treatment protocol for him. Because the tumor was not responsive to chemotherapy, they recommended simultaneous chemo and radiation to enhance the potency. I had pulled all the medical journal articles referencing the type of cancer my dad had, and to date, very few people had survived five years with treatment, and no one had survived beyond five years.

Nick told my dad he wouldn't die of this cancer because his work was not finished here. They created a vast prayer circle for my father, and my dad is more than ten years post–initial diagnosis as I write this. Someone somewhere is doing a research paper on the implausibility of his survival. Now, had you asked me my take on shamans up to that point, I may have said, "Meh, take 'em or leave 'em," but there was no harm. Nick, in particular, seemed to know a thing or two; he was right about my dad, while every science journal was wrong. Did he state my dad's future, and that made it true? Or was it my dad's future, and he was just able to connect to it and know? I dunno. Maybe both. I don't know if it matters, but my mind will always try to figure it out.

When he arrived, he was wearing light-colored clothing and carried his satchel of magic tricks. The quality of his voice stood out—raspy, somewhat spastic—and he had a sense of humor, conveying that we really take our physical selves too seriously. He began by setting up piles of his sage and lighting it on fire to catalyze spirits and cleanse the space, creating enough smoke to fill the downstairs of my parents' large home. He explained the ceremony and what to expect. It all sounded pretty much like your standard shamanistic party, so off we went into the great unknown. He was laughing, saying, "Don't you just love all that smoke?!" while I'm gagging and Mark's asthma is flaring, but who am I to judge? Or interrupt the ancient practice of summoning the other world?

Present at the party were three dudes and me, Nick, my dad, Mark, and Shelby (my dogger), all sitting in a circle in the formal living room. He spoke some words and then asked me to sit on the impromptu ceremonial altar: my mom's massage table, occasionally used for some random Reiki sessions. Justifiably; it was filled with good juju. He asked if I was taking any pharmaceuticals, and I said that I had been on Zoloft for a couple of years. He said, "Get off; that's poison. You need spiritual healing."

He then continued telling me that, in Native American culture, only the strongest women are blessed with the souls that have the shortest journeys, that you are considered special if you are chosen to carry a soul only for a short while. You are chosen to carry those miscarriages because you can handle them; it is revered and thought of as a gift.

What a novel and beautiful way to conceptualize miscarriage! The reframe helped me feel special and chosen to help these souls complete their short journey, instead of the Western narrative which implies that, as a woman, I was broken and maybe the cause of a miscarriage. With this new worldview, I could imagine actually looking forward to helping some short-termers (miscarriages). I could feel my whole being soften, like my head knew it wasn't my fault, but my body didn't—until now. Those babies have their own journey, and they chose me as the vessel for their short karma because they knew I could do it. How healing it was to feel specially selected, and it quickly shifted my perception from a miscarriage as a "problem" to part of the journey.

With that sense of being chosen for my strength came the release of shame bound in the old story. Less shame opened up my capacity to share my story freely. Because in Western culture women who have had miscarriages, stillbirths, and loss are covertly pathologized, we silence our stories. This silence perpetuates shame. I, as a therapist, help clients heal from shame, even while battling my own. I listen to people tell stories that they never felt like they could speak aloud, and I listen without judgment. Having our stories witnessed by others without judgment reduces the shame. As women, we can change our culture around childbearing experiences by telling our whole truths, perhaps first to each other.

Considering miscarriage affects 30 to 35 percent of early pregnancies, it should be an expected part of the process, not an anomaly. Then we could honor the process of childbearing as inviting grace and loss into our lives at the same time, instead of the fantasy that we are just inviting endless joy through pregnancy. That is the fairy-tale story in our culture, right? As a woman, we have children because that is our purpose, and it is all joy, sunshine, and roses. It provides meaning and value to our lives, and the disconnect between that story and the reality causes suffering, tremendous suffering. Suffering is caused by the difference between expectation and actual experience. Until my shaman healing, I almost felt like it was all a setup, where only a few lucky women escape child-rearing without a termination, loss, or miscarriage, and yet, their story is the one we tell to each other about mommahood, especially in mainstream media.

Nick then said, "You will have a daughter . . . first." My attention stuttered at his word choice. I interpreted it to mean that more children were coming our way, but there was this odd pause around "a daughter," and he didn't say anything more.

He finished saging me and giving me his guidance, and I hopped down off the table and joined our makeshift circle. Mark was up next, heh heh. For those who know Mark, he is very "this-worldly." Most of what I am writing in this book, he attributes to mere coincidence and happenstance, firmly grounded in scientific explanation or just random connection. Well, Nick must have known that, because the first thing he said to him as he sat on the table was, "What is wrong with your left shoulder?"

Mark said, "Hmmm, that has been bugging me for a long time."

Then Nick kept going, "What about your right knee?"

Mark replied, "Oh yeah, I just hurt that the other day."

I knew Mark's shoulder had been bothering him, but I didn't know he had tweaked his knee while painting earlier in the week. The only other thing that I remember Nick telling him was, "It's not your fault. Those losses were not your fault." Again, what a gift. His words took away all the conscious and unconscious pressure for both of us.

From that visit, we headed to Puerto Rico. On vacation, we never left the resort, and one evening, trying my hand at roulette, Mark was betting some numbers and colors. I'm not much of a gambler, but I called a couple of good numbers, so the guy next to me said, "What next?"

I said "Double zero," and we all bet. Click, click, click, and the ball slides into zero-zero.

We all cheer, then he says, "What next?"

I say, "Double zero again."

He kind of looks at me with eyes declaring, "That is so unlikely," but for some reason, we all bet zero-zero again, because why not? Click, click, click . . . click . . . click . . . click. Zero-zero.

"Ahhhhhhhh" cheers all around, but I knew when luck had run its course, so we left the table. And how could my intuition win money at roulette but not bring a baby into this world?

Later in the week, it was pouring rain and about seventy degrees, so I dragged Mark out for a beach walk. The beach has always been my place, my safe space, nurturing and healing. We walked until we were drenched, weighted down with twenty pounds of soggy clothes, and when it felt right, I laid down, belly on the sand, rain pounding on my back, and bled my tears of sorrow into the soft, welcoming earth. I sobbed, big whole-body sobs. What if I couldn't have children forever? I released it all into the ground below and allowed my dreads, fears, doubts to be swallowed up by the land that kisses the ocean. Soon, those sorrows could be washed out into the deep for safekeeping.

I recalled Nick's words, "You will have a daughter . . . first," pondered his phrasing again, clutching those words like my purse in Times Square on New Year's Eve. In the coming days, months, and years, any time I questioned whether we would actually be able to have children, I thought back to that day. I couldn't make this journey alone anymore. We are all on our own unique journey, even though we dance and move together. Sure enough, the shaman was right. We got pregnant that March, right after our trip.

Busy with private practice and teaching fitness, Mark was working IT full time, perfecting greens, and finding his voice as an artist. I was continually researching ways to make art a business, not an easy task! Unfortunately, my research generally drummed up one hundred questions and doubts for every one answer.

Painting incessantly, submitting work to competitions, we got big news: Mark won the Grand Prize for best landscape with *International Artist Magazine* and was on the February/March 2010 cover. Each article, each award, blew a little burst of air into the hope hot air balloon bringing the dream of full-time artist back aloft.

I kept looking at other artists' stories, like who Mark admired and how they made it as an artist. Many successful artists had gallery representation, and a few of the most notable artists had studied under Mark's idol, Richard Schmid, who was arguably one of the best living representational artists at the time. Some artists sold work from their home galleries, and many held workshops to help pay the bills. It became apparent to me that all the top artists kind of knew each other. Figuring we needed to start knowing the right people, I started contacting folks. I thought, *What is the worst thing that can happen? No response?*

First on my list was the wife of a big-time Western landscape artist. I emailed her and asked her how they became successful. I contacted her because he was very well known, and they ran a private gallery out of their homestead. She was listed as the gallery contact; they seemed like a team. Soon after, she responded. So stunned that she replied, I archived that email for years. She said all the things I am saying now—that she saw talent in Scott, helped him start a gallery, and ran the gallery while he painted. I began to have a clearer vision for our business future. I work like this a lot, though. I imagine where we will be and then work back from there. See and feel the goal first, then figure out the steps to get there.

I also reached out to Richard Schmid's assistant, because who doesn't just go to the top when looking for answers? Most successful people find mentors, and although Richard groomed artists in the past, he didn't really do that anymore. Unsure of how it could help, but sure it couldn't hurt, the closest I could get Mark to meeting Richard was to sign him up to take a workshop by a well known artist, located at the Putney barn where Richard's painting group, the Putney Painters, met regularly. This group felt so elite. We even heard a story from a woman who relocated entirely from promises to join this little club. It appeared as if his talent could cast a spell, and we needed a little magic for Mark to make it as an artist.

Mark's art career and my work were a distraction through the first trimester, which went smoothly. I was terrified of miscarrying again, so I didn't share with many people that we were expecting. However, the first two ultrasounds at about six and twelve weeks showed that her heartbeat and size were normal, and generally, she seemed to be developing just fine.

Continuing into the second trimester, we opted for some basic genetic testing at eighteen weeks. When the results came back, we got a call from the midwife, and she said that everything looked normal except for this hormone created by the placenta, PAPP-A. The levels were abnormally low.

My heart dropped. Why can't I just have an easy-breezy pregnancy?! At that time, this hormone level was tested in conjunction with many other things to determine the risk of major birth defects, like trisomy and a few other issues. The low levels were an odd outlier. Concerned, we scheduled a full anatomy scan for twenty weeks at the hospital. We had about a three-week wait, and so we waited.

#

Three weeks later, we arrived nervously for our full-body scan appointment. New technician, new office, new procedure. I undressed, and we waited for the doctor. She arrived and said hello somewhat curtly, then gelled up my abdomen to begin wanding my belly. Whenever an ultrasound wand touches my body, my heart pounds and I begin sweating. I looked to the screen of grayness, willing her to show me ten fingers and toes.

The anatomy scan began. Heart looked fine, check. Lungs looked fine, check. All her limbs measured appropriately, check. Spine was formed, check. And her brain looked normal. Phew! Nothing in the scan indicated trisomy, which can cause life-threatening conditions, nor are any other abnormalities detected. As the saying goes, she had ten fingers and toes.

The doctor came in after the scan and said she looked totally normal, with nothing to indicate any issues, but at the end, she paused, looking bewildered. There seemed to be something, but nothing was clearly presenting itself, and she offered no further insight. Regardless, I breathed a sigh of relief; I didn't ask any more questions. She seemed fine, so I didn't want to dwell on things I had no control over. We left the visit, the scan behind us. We just had regular measurement visits scheduled after that, and checkups where they listened to her heartbeat. If you cup your ears with your hands, squeeze, and release your palms against your head, it almost sounds like her heart monitor.

My mom really wanted to have a baby shower, and for some reason, I was resistant to it. I was not feeling up to it, wondering if we could have a shower after the baby was born or something. But the family was so excited that the shower gained its own momentum. We had two—one in Connecticut and one in Missouri. The whole family was ready and waiting for this new baby with great anticipation after three years of trying.

Summer blinked into fall. My body was changing; I could feel her moving around. I continued teaching Nia and ran my private practice full-time. Mark worked and painted, and although expensive for us at the time and competitive, he attended his first workshop in Putney in 2010. I also found out that, on the final day, Richard would paint a still life for the workshop as a live demonstration. I thought to myself, *Okay, I got him to the door; he will have to do the rest.* Mark went to the workshop, and the instructor saw that he was talented and told Richard about him. Richard gave Mark a signed copy of his book, *Alla Prima*, with the note, "Mark—Joy to you and your art. Share it freely and it will come back to you in more ways than you can imagine. Your friend, Richard Schmid. 2010." Another feather in Mark's cap, a solid message to keep going from one of the greatest.

With all this momentum, there was almost nothing that would make me doubt we were on our way to a full-time art business and soon-to-be family. Our goals were so close! Then, one night in the basement, for whatever reason, Mark was describing an object's color using terms like "gray" when I saw it as "green." I thought Mark's way of talking about color was quirky, so in jest, I asked him to take this colorblindness test online. He logged on to humor me and started clicking through the images, the tiny dots of one color with a number or letter of dots made up of another color.

Guess what? He freaking failed the red/green assessment! I lost my mind! What are you saying? You can't see red/green? How did you not know? Why did you choose art if you are colorblind? Spinning twisted thoughts trying to make sense of this new information. I called his mom, and his mom said something like, "Oh yeah, I vaguely recall something about that from elementary school."

I just have no answers here. I do not know to this day how he ever pursued painting. Representational painting is about good drawing and expertise in reproducing values in hues. I imagine it occurs on a spectrum, but no, Mark cannot see the circles making up the red six amid the green dots. Until then, we had never spoken of Mark's color-seeing deficit, but I imagined it was unlikely that someone with these challenges would find success in fine art. Where there was a "yes," there always seemed to be a "no," as well, so it was essential to refocus on the yeses and not ask Mark to spot the red fall leaves amid a green landscape.

Soon, we would have a newborn, so the pressure to figure out how this art thing was going to work intensified. Visits and measurements of the growing baby were normal, but everyone kept telling me how small I looked. Finally, around week thirty-two, I went in for a visit and told the doctor that everyone said I was looking so small. She noted that all pregnancies are different and kind of brushed it off. I taught fitness and was petite, so that was the explanation that satisfied her. In that visit, I measured between one and two centimeters small with the tape measure, and she said, "Well if you measure small again, we will do an ultrasound in your next visit in two weeks."

Not knowing any different, I said, "Okay," and left the visit.

A few days later, I started to have pain on my left side that felt like a kidney stone. I had had one a few years earlier, and it felt familiar. It was after hours on a Friday evening, and I wanted to avoid an ER visit if I could, so I called the on-call doctor and described my pain. Without any other symptoms, I explained what it felt like and how I thought it was a kidney stone. She said, "If it is a kidney stone, there is nothing to be done," and the ER was really busy, so she recommended waiting it out at home. So I did. The pain seemed manageable, so I went to sleep, and when I woke up, it seemed better. I will never know if that pain was related to what came next, but it is one of those moments that haunts me, because I often recall it and wonder, *What if?* What if I had gone to the hospital that night? Five days later, the following Wednesday, I met her: my messenger, the owl. November 17, 2010.

11

Sophie Joy's Birth, Death, And Decisions

Burlington, Vermont: 2010

The day is etched in my memory like a fossil in the Alaskan ice shelf. It is cold, it is gritty, and it won't budge. Although, I guess now even the ice shelf is melting and shifting, so maybe eventually my emotional memory will, too. Memories are malleable; we tend to remember things in the present that reflect our current feeling state, and the details around memories change over time based on how we make sense of our experience. After the age of four, we can make cognitive memories, narratives of events, and prior to that, everything is just stored as emotional memories, which are sensations in our bodies. We continue to store emotions as sensations throughout our lives. Every day, body sensations can be about the present and the past at the same time. As our relationship to an event changes, so can our recollections of what happened and the associated emotional memories, so our body sensations may change, too. Perhaps not this one. Some of these moments are imprinted, solid, unwavering, and that is okay, because I opted for no photos.

A photoshoot was offered, among other ways of memorializing her, most of which I found traumatizing. Once you see something, you can't unsee it. This visual memory becomes something that I could recall over and over again. It attaches itself to an emotional memory, a sensation in my body, and I didn't want that. I was very conscious of the visual memories that might stay deeply connected to the emotional heartache of that day.

The one thing I told myself over and over when we went to the hospital to deliver her was: *Only I know how to get through this, only I can make choices today that feel good for me, and one day from now, one year from now, a lifetime from now, I will know that I will never again be that mom having to make such challenging parental decisions for our firstborn.* I now know that was, and still is, true. Although the details of the day are so vivid, the pain has changed, and I will never again be that grieving mom in that moment, so I can't look back and say, "I would have done this or that differently," because I am no longer that mom. I was no longer her the moment I left the hospital. She died that day, too, in a way.

For me, one of the complicated issues about grieving her was that she was my first. I did not have any living children, so I had no context for what I had really lost—nothing concrete in my experience, just what I imagined it would be like to watch her grow up. My grieving was not for a person, per se—because I knew her and I didn't know her—but only for the life that I had imagined for her. I was grieving a dream for the future, not memories from the past. That's the other funny thing about thinking: It is either about the past or future. Only sensing and feeling occur in the present moment. In technical terms, they call this kind of grief "complicated"—well, thanks for that "clarification!" Yes, it is totally complicated.

It is weird and unbearable and impossible to live through, and yet we all did it, and we still are. I think one of the scary parts of having gone through something so awful is the reality that life can really get that bad. Mark and I had a joke after her death where one of us would say, "It can't get any worse," and the other would say, "Oooh yes, yes it can." There really is no rock bottom to the pain that we may endure as physical humans on this earth, and that reality was paralyzing to me for a long time after her birth. Because I had listened to so many others' stories, I knew that life could get challenging, but I hadn't felt it. Her death awakened a depth of grief and sorrow that was unimaginable until I was in it. I knew I could feel sad and tortured and physical pain, but that was abstract compared to burying my unborn child.

The doctors encouraged me to go home after the ultrasound and sit with the news and check into the hospital when I was ready, but I had no desire to wait any longer at home. Feeling an internal pressure to get this all over with as soon as I could, we went to the hospital right away. Her soul was gone. It was creepy and sad, and I wanted to get through delivery as quickly as possible, but that was all out of my control. Stopping home to gather a few things before driving to the hospital, I felt sick to my stomach, blankness in my mind, like floating in and out of pure dread, staring down the events that were to come over the next day.

I checked into Labor and Delivery at the hospital and was given a room surrounded by moms having healthy babies. I can hear labor and delivery sounds, like crying babies, moms in joy and pain, and movement around the corridor. I want to walk, I want to move, but I don't dare leave this cocoon for fear of what I might see: happy moms. Happy moms felt like facing Freddy Krueger in my dreams. They tried to put me away from others as much as possible, but I could still hear the sounds of new life all around me. They attached a black ribbon to the door so everyone entering knew this was a loss and not a live birth. It was almost as if the pain hung in the air of my hospital room, and as every nurse entered, she took a breath, filling her lungs with despair, and exhaled into the sadness with me. Recalling the room, the people, the somatic memory of the grief announces herself with the sensation of getting punched in the stomach, an aching in my heart, and warm bubbling of tears.

For the first few hours at the hospital, we hung out with my parents and started adjusting to this new reality that we were no longer expecting a baby in our lives. Consumed with emotional pain, I had moments of coherent thought, like, *Who do I call? And how do I tell them this news?* Because it is so awful, I just couldn't even face saying the words "she died" out loud. My life was reasonably public as a fitness instructor with many students, as a therapist with many clients, along with friends and family. I needed people to know, because I would be putting everything on hold for the time being. So, I decided to call two friends, Sarah and Nevin, and asked that they let people know the news. I also rang my supervisor and left a message. The energy required to make those three phone calls was like climbing Everest with no oxygen tanks—suffocating. I couldn't bear telling one more person, afraid of their potential reaction; it just seemed to amplify my own. Even calling those few close friends, the absolute shock could be felt through the phone as I tried to tell them she was gone. All the while, nurses and doctors filed in and out, checking vitals, taking blood, and running tests. I kept thinking, *Maybe they are all wrong. Maybe when I deliver her, she will start breathing.* Ah, hope—she is an optimistic friend—but I guess that momentary thought gave me relief from the impenetrable sadness, if only for a second.

The first anesthesiologist entered and introduced herself, and unfortunately left a lasting impression for the worst reasons: She was a good ole fashioned advice giver. She wanted to chat with me about my plans for after delivery, even though she was primarily involved in medicating me before and during the procedure. She had been through this before with other patients, so she wanted to share everything she knew. "Do you plan to spend time with the baby after she is born?" she asked, as well as "Do you have a name for her or plan to name her?" These concerns felt essential to her, like my answers to those questions would determine the ease of my grief. I disagreed.

Hearing her questions was like walking through a hailstorm, each piece drumming itself against my tired body, leaving me more dented and bruised. I didn't really know my answers for sure, but to this point, we hadn't named her, and I wasn't sure I wanted to spend time with the body. I can't unsee the body, but I can always imagine what she might have looked like as a vibrant soul, and I wanted to keep that memory intact, because it felt like a warm, fuzzy memory instead of a shocking, sad one.

"I'm not sure I can handle holding the body of a baby whose spirit is already gone; it's just her body to me, nothing more," I responded.

My response invited more well-meaning advice: "Well, I have known women who do not hold their babies, and they regret it, but I have never known a mom who regrets spending time with her baby after it died." So again, thank you for the unsolicited advice, and I have some advice for you: Stay in your lane, lady; tell me about the drugs! I didn't say that out loud, but I wanted to.

Instead, I moved the conversation on to ways I might be totally unconscious for the birth, like knocked out, and I asked to deliver by C-section. My brilliant plan wasn't really an option, because the risks are too significant. I guess no doctor wants to put someone under if it isn't essential. Ugh! *How does anyone do this?* I thought to myself. Plan B was giving me enough pain medication that I wouldn't feel the birth at all, and I could even take something that would cause amnesia afterward, so I wouldn't remember it. I focused on Plan B: enough medication to numb a small farm animal, zero pain. The epidural with Pitocin was ordered to begin labor.

Explaining the procedure, she said they would inject my spine with a numbing agent first and then insert the epidural, which is like a small tube drip. It is a bit of an art, because they must place it perfectly, which is different for everyone. And with all medical procedures, there is a slight risk; this one is paralysis. It was like adding salt to an open wound, one procedure talk after another with each doctor, hearing something like, "This usually goes well buuuttt there is this one risk." My weary mind kept repeating, *Why can't they just knock me out?*

Her comments, like other parts of this awful journey, were jarring and not helpful. That is the thing about trauma—the more emotionally negative the experience, the more strongly it is imprinted on our nervous systems. The emotional memory gets stored as sensations in the body, and for survival, we are way better at remembering the shitty parts of life than the joyful ones. After forty years of life on this planet, I have realized how important it is to practice JOY, PEACE, and SERENITY, because I need so much more of those experiences to counteract my propensity to remember the challenging ones. Joy is a practice for me; it doesn't just happen. So, the anesthesiologist, unfortunately, holds a significant place in the imagery of that day for me, and she wasn't the only anesthesiologist that locked herself in the tragedy—so did the one who came post–shift change.

The nurses streamed in, checking my vitals, making sure I was comfortable, and my in-laws arrived. They offered that I might call Jenn, my sister-in-law, because she had been through something similar years before. Jaw drop. I had no idea. How had I not known? I called Jenn, bless Jennifer; she said, "I am going to tell you things no one else is going to tell you. I am going to tell you what to expect and things that will happen, like your milk coming in, that will help you make all the decisions you need to." She explained how they got the news that their child in between their two daughters would not survive outside the womb, and they decided to terminate later in pregnancy. She was my lifeline I didn't even know I had, someone I knew well that had been through this already. I didn't have to figure it all out, just some of it, on my own.

My body kept flashing hot and cold. At times, it felt surreal; I would cry, talk, cry, and laugh. One nurse noted, "You are handling this so well." I wondered what that even meant. What does it mean to handle tragedy well? I kind of looked forward to the drugs, so I wouldn't have to handle anything anymore. This is when dissociation is really helpful, and lucky me—I'm all trained up on staying in my body, so it isn't really an option for me. It is hard for me to dissociate from my body.

A doctor came in to see if I was already in labor.

"Are you having any contractions?"

I reply, "No."

She checks dilation, looks at me, and says, "You are over two centimeters dilated, and you aren't having contractions?"

I said, "No," no clue my body had started labor, thinking, *Am I supposed to know?*

For whatever reason, I verbally bombarded the next nurse that entered with my owl story, the whole event spilling out of me—how the owl greeted me the day before, and how it felt like she had an important message. The nurse was mesmerized, and after checking my vitals, left only to return a few minutes later with numerous pages she had printed off from researching the internet.

She handed them to me and said, "You will never believe this." They all described the meaning and symbolism of the owl. She was so excited and teary, she said, "Do you know that the owl is commonly known to visit to ferry the dead to the afterlife?" I still get chills.

"No, I had no idea, but I just felt like I had to tell you my story for some reason," I replied.

"In Native American culture, owls are known to be harbingers of death, an omen," whispered my new nurse friend.

Before that moment, even though I had gone on owl walks with Audoboners as a kid, I had never seen an owl in nature. I now knew the meaning of seeing into those eyes: They were connected to her, my daughter. She stopped for a minute shortly after her death to let me know she was on her way. Those eyes, her owl eyes, would be the only time I saw my daughter on this earth. That is one of the ways I remember her and how she looked.

It gives me warm fuzzies, not prickly stings, like seeing her after birth might have. Telling my owl story on impulse to that nurse that evening gave me the gift of the meaning of her visit. Many years later, giving a talk about our daughter and the owl, a gentleman on in his years came up to me after the talk and tearfully shared that, many years ago, his wife had lost many children. When they finally moved from their house into a new one, they went to take down a tree, and in it were a few baby owls. He had a new relationship to his owls from that day on and found it healing.

Evening rose around us, nurses in and out, waiting, more waiting. Around 6 or 7 p.m., I was visited by the second anesthesiologist. He was loud, boisterous, and boomed his introduction from halfway across the room. Alongside him was the intern who would administer the epidural.

I thought to myself, *Why do they let the intern do the most complex part? Why? How many has he done before me?* I wanted no mistakes, but there never is a 100 percent guarantee in life, not even when they offer it in the commercials. The lackey came around behind me while the head dude watched. He said, "Okay, big stick." Ow, fuck me, ow, jeeezus, ow, and I squeezed Mark's hands and breathed. It starts to feel a little numb. He pulled out the needle, said, "Okay, I'm putting in the epidural," and then inserted it. Procedure, done. Another step in the delivery journey, done. I kept mentally checking off the boxes for each step I successfully complete toward the end goal: baby delivery.

The anticipation was as bad as each present moment.

The doctors all scurried out, and I was left with Mark to wait. They started the drip to numb the lower half of my body and would later add Pitocin to initiate contractions. I felt no change, no numbness, nothing. Another nurse, doctor, intern, not sure, flew in to insert a catheter. I told her I wasn't numb and that I could feel everything that she was doing.

She said, "You shouldn't be able to feel anything."

I said, "I'm not numb at all; I can feel it."

She responded, "It will only be a minute," and inserted the catheter. I cried; I had no stamina for any more pain. We waited.

I was still not feeling numb, so I told Mark to let someone know I could still feel the lower half of my body. The anesthesiologist came in and turned up the medication. We waited. I started to feel a warm wave moving from my waist upward, slowly creeping through my chest and back, up to my neckline. I thought to myself, *Don't panic, breathe.* The warmth blossomed into numbness; I was numb from the waist up, not the waist down. Now, I started to panic. *What if the drugs make it impossible to breathe? Or stop my heart? What in the actual fuck?*

"Mark, go get the doctor right now!" I said while internally, jaw clenched, telling myself to stay calm, much like asking a screaming toddler to finish his broccoli—saying words that land nowhere.

The intern came back, and I told him I was numb from my waist up to my neck and could feel my body from my waist down.

"That's weird; that has never happened before," he casually responds.

My internal tantrum screams, *Google it, dude! Don't tell me you have never encountered it before! This is my life you are fucking with! Do you realize this is the worst day of my life?! You are making it even worse, asshole!*

He tilted my bed slightly to elevate my head more and said, "Try that," and left the room. He was lucky he didn't get too close; I might have bit him at that moment, crazed with grief and fear. After a few minutes, still no change. Finally, Mark adjusted my bed so that I was almost standing, like holding on to the rails, so I didn't slide down off the cot like a slippery, wet noodle. And then, sweet relief. The numbness in my chest began to drain to the right places. I guess, bless their souls, although not funny at the time, they now provide comic relief to that day; they all had their purpose.

More waiting.

It is late evening now. I just wanted to deliver this baby as fast as possible and leave the hospital, but the evening ticked on, no change, nothing. We waited, and our parents had left. I couldn't feel any contractions, so I guess that was a plus. Mark and I were left with ourselves in that hospital room, mostly in silence. What do you say? I usually have a lot of words, but in those hours, I had none. Anything I could say seemed like futile attempts to help pass time; my words had no meaning. As nurses came in and out, I asked if we could move things along, but they told me it would be a while. I guess it was a busy night for delivering babies, and I was at the end of the waitlist.

Now, if you are wondering why the twelve-hour wait? Me fucking too. The delay in delivery to this day baffles me. I guess they have more pressing birthing moms and babies, but the waiting is the equivalent of sustained water torture. The pastor, the social worker, and the nurses flitted in and out, asking questions about logistics like death/birth certificates, naming, memorial services, plans for the body, autopsy, counseling, photos, and memory boxes. The hospital creates a memory box that includes the hat and booties they put on the baby after delivery, plus a lock of hair if the baby has hair. They will also take photos and arrange for that if I want it; I said no. The memory box seems thoughtful, but all that stuff was from her death, not her life; I said no.

The nurse said, "Well, no matter what you say today, we keep it for a week, in case you change your mind." I see how well-intentioned this is, but it fills me with rage. I don't want the stupid memory box that was some social worker's "good idea" implemented to ease the pain for something they probably never felt. And if they keep a lock of her hair in a box for a week, and then I don't come back to get it, I still know it is sitting there, and then I feel guilty for not taking it. Even though I didn't want it to be, the box was created, and then not taking it feels like somehow I am not remembering or honoring her correctly. Their reasoning for keeping the box for a week was that so many women return to pick up the keepsake after they leave, and so they felt validated in making the decision for me to "hold on to it" in case I change my mind. I thought, *Yeah, maybe sometimes women come back to get it after because they feel guilty.*

Unsolicited advice, decisions being made about memorializing our daughter—it all made me feel more powerless. I imagine everyone I encountered felt as helpless as I did that day. Usually, when we feel powerless, we want to help. I do, too, generally, but becoming a helper in the face of someone else's emotional tragedy is actually not helpful at all. In therapy, I practice a lot of holding space for what is, which means tolerating my discomfort in the face of another's pain, not trying to fix it or offer suggestions for how to fix it, but just allowing myself to be with it in relationship to the other person. I appreciate, though, that medical staff is not trained in the depths of trauma psychotherapy, but when everyone around me was trying to help my emotional pain by offering advice or making decisions "just in case," I just continued to feel more and more powerless.

See, my baby dying, that was totally out of my control. She had her own path, like the shaman perhaps predicted, and I had no control over that, even though it was all happening in my body. What I did have control over was listening to my intuition to guide me through and making my own decisions at each point of the delivery. But when my desires and other people's advice did not match up, I felt guilty and questioned myself. It was disempowering to have doctors and nurses tell me what they thought might be best. When others offer advice unintentionally, it puts the advice giver, the "knower," in a position of power, and you, the receiver, in a position of powerlessness. I was repeatedly put in a position of powerlessness throughout her birth.

Powerlessness and fear are the seat of trauma, along with shame and guilt. The way that we begin to heal from trauma is by regaining a sense of empowerment, and my intuition was already telling me how to heal. I just had to listen, but it meant blocking out all the noise of well-intentioned advice and doing things my own way, even if it was different than the way most others did it. It was a lot of mind chess for my weary heart, trying to sift through decisions.

There is a lot of implicit pressure to do things like name your child. Even though they say you don't have to, they asked me repeatedly, despite me saying no. I felt strongly that her name would come to me if it was supposed to, and though it hadn't yet, it did come to me in a dream a few weeks later.

The nurses asked how I wanted the room for delivery, and I wanted it dark and quiet. I told them I'd like peaceful music, and that after I delivered, I'd like her body moved to another room. I felt so judged, but I rolled with it anyway.

Finally, around 2 a.m., the midwife that I know the best from the OB practice, the one who had given us the low PAPP-A results, was there to deliver our daughter. I cried tears of relief when I saw it was her; she was the only practitioner from the practice that I felt like I knew to a degree. She had stayed on past her shift to help us, a true act of service.

It was dark and quiet, and she explained how delivery unfolds. She said, "Bear down to push," and we began. Mark at my side, I couldn't look him in the eye. It felt like I might drown in the ocean of his sad blue eyes.

I told him, "Just hold my hand, and whatever you do, do not let go of my hand, do not let go." I closed my eyes and focused on my work ahead as a mom, keeping half of my attention on his tight grip.

After a few simple pushes and twenty minutes, she was out. Kristen said, "She's small, and she has a full head of dark hair." I cried. I had elected to allow an autopsy to find out more about what happened and potentially explain why she was tiny and why the placenta looked unusual. Nurses whisked her out into a side room wrapped in blankets and a cap, just like if she were born breathing. I cried, I wailed, I breathed relief. One more step in this horrible process was done, check.

Mark left to go see her, and I let him be the eyes for us all. I rested and breathed deep. I asked the nurses if I could leave now, as in go home. They told me I needed to wait. I was ready to leave. I needed out of this hospital.

My arguments weren't too convincing. I closed my eyes to rest into a druggy, half-conscious haze while nurses came in to check on me, removing all the tubes. I asked Mark what she looked like, and he said, "She looks like me."

I asked, "Is she blue?"

He said, "Yeah."

I said again, "I can't see her; I won't be able to unsee her."

After three hours of lying in bed, waiting for the clock to hit a reasonable a.m. hour, Mark in a makeshift bed lying next to me, the sun began winking over the mountains. I think to myself, *Thank goddess her delivery is over. Thank goddess I am waking up on the other side of that horrendous, soul-crushing work. I made it.*

In the midst of preparing for delivery, we were faced with choices about what to do with her body, and these were like *forever* choices. If we bury her, do we get a casket? Have a funeral? How do I plan a funeral in my current state? What would they say during a service? I didn't really know her as a personality, only as a person to be in my life. Would we get her a plot? If she had a headstone, would I visit her? What if we just skip the funeral and bury her, but then I never want to go to her plot, and then I know the gravesite is there, but I never go? Will that make me feel guilty? What are the best decisions I can make to honor her that won't torture my existence for all my waking days to come?

I couldn't, in that moment, make any decision that I thought would bring me more pain, and yet, there was no way to know for sure. All there was was the limitless advice of doctors, nurses, a pastor, family, and friends. But truth be told, no one really knows what to do, not even me. I didn't know then, and I still don't know if we made "the right" choices now, but I rest in the fact that they were the "right choices in that moment." At times I wonder, *Should I have spent time with her body?* But to this day, I do not regret it. I don't love her any less because I didn't hold her body; I just never had a relationship with her physical body, and that works for me.

Mark and I decided before leaving the hospital to have her cremated and buried in the hospital memorial dedicated to unborn and newly born babies that don't survive. They hold a memorial service once or twice a year in honor of all of these babies. The next ceremony wasn't until spring, so I figured we had time to decide if we wanted to attend. To this day, we haven't. SJ was not ours to keep, nor was her body, but our spiritual connection is represented by the owl. For many years, I wore owl earrings and necklaces and a wing necklace all the time, which is how I kept her close. I had to find my own way to be in relationship with SJ.

As I reflect, it feels odd to me that I felt like there was a right way to do things that day, like I could sense what was expected of me in the hospital—some weird pressure to fit in and follow the "normal" way to do things in terms of managing the death of a baby. I'm here to say, though, there is no normal. Losing a baby is not "normal," but it is a part of motherhood, the bit we don't often talk about.

It almost feels like a toxic relationship in a way, like when I work with clients who return again and again to people who are physically and emotionally abusive. There is often an absolute ability to split the experience of "good" and "bad" in a partner, so when the abusive partner is acting "dreamy," one can generally "forget" in a way, totally block out the pain from the prior abuse, and experience their partner in the present as all-loving, until the next round. It is almost like, as a culture, we do that with motherhood, and what is accepted is that pregnancy, birth, and what comes after is a magical, blissful joy that is unmatchable. But the reality is perhaps all of that, none of that, or everything in between. What about just ho-hum motherdom? Like parts of it are okay, some fun, some really hard, and a lot of grief? Somehow, we create a fairy tale around motherhood as the pathway to meaning and eternal happiness, and at times it is this, though times it is many other things, too. Our job as moms is to hold it all, tell it all, so we prepare the next generation of moms.

I have so much compassion for parents with sick babies and kids. The death of a child is just one aspect of that type of grief. Some kids are born with challenges that require support for their entire lives, or sometimes kids get sick with severe diseases, and then parenting becomes helping children with pain. I'm only naming a few instances here, but it is all part of parenting, not just the fantasy of quietly nursing your new, full-term, healthy infant at home that sleeps through the night. No, it is life, love, death, sickness, illness, joy, grief, rage, and fear all rolled in one.

Before we could check out, they sent in the social worker again to talk about grief support and remind me that I could change my mind about what to do with the body for up to a week or so. In strides, the doctor who I consulted with the weekend before regarding my severe side pain, the one who encouraged me or supported me in staying home instead of coming in, arrived to apologize for my loss. Standing eye to eye, the rage inside swarmed like a tornado of nails swirling under my skin, fighting to be unleashed in some fury on this young doctor, but I just stared at her and asked if I could leave now, restraining my storm with the last ounce of energy in my frail body.

I was done. I needed to be away from this place and all the experts in it who couldn't save my baby. I walked out, and slowly, step by step, made the roughly half-mile trek through the corridors to the front door. In hindsight, had I known it was a 5K to the exit, I would have taken the wheelchair ride. My one regret from that day!

Our parents picked us up and took us home. I thought I had made it through the worst, and in some ways, I had—the shock, the horror of finding out her heart had stopped, the delivery—but the days and weeks after were full of deep sadness and depression. There were days that I would just tell myself that I did not have to understand anything, did not have to try to make sense of it; all I had to do was breathe. Grief is lonely work, but you can't do it alone.

12

Healing Begins Back In The Chair

Burlington, Vermont: 2011

I did it. I survived that day, her birth date. I got through each step that declared itself and was left feeling guilt and relief that it was over. Guilt because I wanted to rush through that day as fast as possible, and solace that I never had to live that day ever again.

The sun and moon performed their duet of more dark, less light, moving deeper toward the solstice, and my body, like the rhythms of the shortening days, also felt more dark than light. From head to toe, I ached with overwhelming physical pain, as if every cell was being squeezed by vice grips clamping down to gain a little more leverage. It hurt to lie down, sit up, move, cough, talk, so initially, I chose a lot of not moving and not talking. The aching in my heart squeezed like a heart attack, as if I might actually die from grief; my heart might just stop and freeze solid at any moment.

The heart can actually slow almost to death in anticipation that death is imminent. The autonomic nervous system, the part of our nervous system that functions without our conscious effort—breathing, heart rate, digestion, immunity, things like that—has two branches. The sympathetic and parasympathetic branches. And within the parasympathetic branch, there is dorsal vagal and ventral vagal activation of the vagus nerve, which controls heart rate variability and breathing in response to safety or perceived threat. The ventral vagal system is activated and puts the breaks on the dorsal vagal and sympathetic nervous system when we feel relaxed, calm, social—able to play and be in nature. The dorsal vagal system is activated when we are petrified, almost as if preparing for death, and it looks like shut down, withdrawal, feeling really small.

In my initial stages of grief, much later, I came to realize I was in some kind of dorsal vagal state, shut down and immobile. Within this state, the body is not efficient at cellular repair, immunity, digestion, thinking, or higher levels of executive function, which is why profound, long states of stress can exacerbate and cause physical illness and inhibit learning or working. Deep grief felt like this in my body—a collapse, a shutdown, hiding in my cave of covers—and if I stayed there still enough, long enough, I might be consumed by it.

That feeling of not being able to move, physical pain, withdrawal was my body's response to the trauma of losing our daughter and living through her birth. Trauma isn't an event, per se. It was my overwhelming emotional response to losing her, all the intolerable grief, powerlessness, and sadness that was traumatic. Whether it is the death of a loved one, slipping and falling on ice, a car accident, someone calling me a name, surviving a tsunami . . . it is my emotional response to the event that makes it trauma, the emotional overwhelm that imprints itself in my body as a sensation memory. And it is unique to each of us. One person may live through a car accident and never think about it again, while another person may live through a car accident and tense every time she gets in a car. We can never truly predict how we will emotionally respond to trauma, whether we will remain calm and focused, fight, flee, or dissociate—those are our only options, really. Trauma is the series of stories of emotional overwhelm in our lives, not the actual events, and we all have them. SJ is one of mine.

For a few days after her birth, I would wake up, feel empty, feel my body changing, and wonder how the sun could rise. How could the days keep marching on while I was so sad? And yet, some relief that time didn't care about me, the sunrise was bigger than my sadness—there was comfort in that. There is a rhythm to the universe, the world, the days and nights that carry on, and that rhythm carried me for weeks when I couldn't carry myself. Mark and my in-laws were around, but I felt like all of this happened inside my body, so although they would comfort me, I felt like no one could really feel what I was feeling. It was lonely, and yet I somehow wanted others to feel sad with me but knew they couldn't really know my sadness.

No one else had the same relationship to SJ that I did. No one else carried her for nine months, and no one else was her mother. I was the only one. With other losses, like my grandmother, there were many grandchildren, so there were many of us grieving losing a grandmother. Or even a child that has lived—that child may have had more than one caregiver, but I was alone in my relationship to knowing SJ, because she only lived in me. Even so, having immediate family around was reassuring, and I would float into hanging out with them, to lying in bed, and back to hiding under my covers, wishing all the pain would disappear. I had to have time alone, and although being alone felt painful, it was less suffocating than being in a room of everyone's grief that felt different than mine. We were each suffering the loss of a baby, but grieving very different things in a way. Because our relationship to what happened was all different, so was the level of trauma, even for Mark and me.

Mark and I were grieving differently, and although we were in it together, we weren't. It was my body that went through everything, my body that held her, my body that felt her, my body that carried her short life. He expressed that this whole experience all felt surreal to him, and he did not have the same attachment to the pregnancy that I did. He was sad and disappointed, but it was different than the deep hole of emptiness that I felt or the unrelenting powerlessness that somehow, I should have known how to save her, because it was my body. I guess I attribute that to our personalities, experiences, and the physical aspect of carrying a child, but, in reality, we are just all different. No two moms and no two dads grieve alike, and sometimes I think this can create a strain in a partnership.

At the time, I didn't judge it and did not feel the need to have him grieve my way, nor did he attempt to have me do anything differently. We were both free to do it our own way, in a sense. One day in that first week of mourning, he ventured off into the woods to paint the tree where the owl sat during our visit. I believe that was his movement; painting is the way that he moves his feelings. That painting floats around somewhere to this day, a craggy, old, forgettable tree in the woods, too near an airport for habitable living. The meaning of that tree—an event, an artifact, a conversation—is always more important than the actual thing. I think that is why some say making meaning of trauma and loss helps the healing process.

The cards and flowers started to arrive daily at my house, from near and dear friends to long-lost acquaintances. The love and support that showed up on my doorstep overnight was enough to make me believe in magic and fairies; I didn't even know that I knew that many people. Flowers would arrive, and I would have Mark save the card for me to read later when I had the energy and then put the flowers in the garage.

There was something about fresh-cut flowers. The flowers were beautiful and alive, simultaneously dying. Somehow, I didn't want to witness the transition from gorgeous, colorful blossoms to brown, dried, lifeless stalks. Also, these flowers were alive, and she wasn't; it seemed cruel and unjust. They lived out their quiet, short lives in the garage, but I relished and saved every note and card.

Aside from the sheer number of deliveries, what surprised me more was the frequency each note or phone call was filled with another woman's story of a similar loss. I learned more about my family and friend's childbearing years than ever before. I was shocked to hear people I had known my whole life had experienced a baby dying from SIDS, or a late-term loss, loss of a child, miscarriage, or stillbirth. Anecdotally, I knew of two other women who had a stillborn child within a week of my own within my network of family and friends.

So many women, and with each story, I gained strength. If this courageous woman that I knew went on to lead a fulfilling life after loss, so could I. Any moment that I just felt like I couldn't do it anymore, I could not physically stand the grief, I thought about these women in my life and how they had survived the same type of loss, and in fact, thousands of women before me had survived, too.

How many mothers on this planet lose unborn, young, and adult children? It is actually part of the burden of motherhood for many, and that gave me strength and hope. Each story, because most of them were from the past, showed me how life moved on from these profound, dark moments, and that thriving was still a possibility. I actually was not alone. It gave me hope that I wouldn't feel this way forever. I wouldn't hibernate in my den of pillows and sheets forever. It would change. Somehow, focusing on the temporariness of my grief also brought me relief. Change is inevitable.

I was so surprised at how common loss was to so many women, yet I had never heard about it until my own. Women are warriors, we are fierce, we allow ourselves to be open to the most vulnerable depths of pain anyone can experience in this lifetime and still go on to live meaningful, joyful lives.

A little less than a week later, Thanksgiving made her annual visit, but I had no desire to celebrate. We decided the least painful thing to do was to change scenery, so Mark and I drove the four hours south to my parent's home in Connecticut. Change of scenery? Yes. Change of daily activity? No. I laid in the bed in my old room for four days straight, briefly coming down to eat on occasion. Everything blurred together, day to night, awake to asleep, emptiness to sadness, and continued to feel like if I couldn't face anyone but couldn't be alone, I needed people around but not too much. Nothing I did satisfied the swollen ache, and sleep was only a brief reprieve from the cloud of grief choking me. By Sunday, I was ready to go back home, and something in me was prepared to start moving again, grief cloaked and all.

Early that week, I reached out to a somatic practitioner to start some therapy. She was a yogi from a studio I had taught in years before and did not have a psychotherapy background, which I appreciated. She worked solely through the body. The grief was beginning to feel heavy and stuck, and something in me was telling me, "Move, you need to move," so I hoped she would be able to help me.

Every morning, I began to get out of bed intentionally and make myself get up and drink my coffee. When I started to feel a wave of sadness rise up, instead of collapsing, I would put on music that intensified it, and I would dance it until the surge retreated. I would not stop until I could feel it let go of its grip on my soul. I would move into the pain and let it be whatever bigness it needed to be. Then I would move on with small daily tasks: walking, eating, caring for my dog, watching TV, reading—small, regular-life types of responsibilities that did not require too much mentally. The moments where I felt stuck, like I couldn't possibly move, I started a new recipe. I would give myself a time limit, ten to twenty minutes to lay in my bed and hide from the world, and then I would make myself get up and go to the store or work on a Nia routine, but I literally made my body move. I would tell myself, *Wanting to move and moving are not the same thing; my feelings about moving and actually getting out of bed are not the same thing.* And day by day, moving became a little easier. It was a very physical process, and the mental challenge was making myself move.

At the root level, trauma affects our nervous system, our biochemistry, and all systems like immunity, metabolism, and digestion. When I was healing, I kept forcing myself to move, and movement is an essential part of sympathetic activation, as well as ventral vagal activation, but not the collapse of dorsal vagal activation. In fact, to move out of dorsal vagal collapse, one has to activate the sympathetic nervous system, but I didn't know this at the time. All I knew was that I had to keep moving. That was the message: Allow yourself to collapse for a few minutes, maybe even an hour, but then get moving. Making myself move, whether it was taking a shower, focusing on breathing, dancing or walking, was a forced activation of the sympathetic nervous system. In fact, it was the only way back to emotional balance.

As mentioned earlier, EMDR supports healing, somehow through cross-lateral stimulation through eye movement, tapping, walking, etc., and can help regulate the emotional body. Along with that, I later learned that to move out of a dorsal vagal collapse, a shutdown place, we must activate the sympathetic nervous system, which is the branch of our nervous system that prepares us for fighting or fleeing, before we can then achieve a regulated, ventral vagal state. The sympathetic branch is active in conflict, when we feel ignored or fidgety, but in positive ways, the sympathetic branch is also activated during exercise and play. The eye movement during my most distressing times, through dance, walking, etc., not only triggered my fight/flight sympathetic response, but also began to alleviate the overwhelm of grief. It began to reprogram the memory with a more regulated emotional state.

Within those first few weeks, a dear friend brought over some food and told me we would sit Shiva for SJ, so we did. We ate, drank, and sat Shiva. We talked about how much it all sucked, we spoke of other deaths—there was nothing off the table for discussion and nothing too scary to talk about. Upon reflection, aside from the gift of Shiva, the awesomeness in that visit was that she just did it—she took the lead. When others are in grief, we often ask, "What can I do?" but sometimes the pain is so deep that the griever doesn't know the answer. Still, as grievers, we need something, anything to help. Also, that thinking part of our brain, the prefrontal cortex, is not online when we are in overwhelming emotional states of fear, guilt, shame, and powerlessness. From her, I learned that when someone is grieving, just plan and sit Shiva with them, even though I'm not Jewish.

Whether we heal from trauma or carry the experience with us in the form of a body memory depends on whether we could get regulated after the event through social engagement. Often, as children, the trauma isn't from the overwhelming experience itself, but the fact that we endured the immense feelings all alone when we didn't actually have the neurobiology to handle it. My healing was possible because I was surrounded by family, friends, and community that shared my grief in moments when I couldn't carry it alone. Being in relationship with other people is what helps our own nervous systems find balance—ventral vagal dominance.

Co-regulation happens because of attunement through nonverbals, like eye contact, body posture, and even mirror neurons. If I am with someone who is angry or sad, my nervous system will mimic facial expression or body tension, so, in essence, I feel what the other person is feeling. Mirroring is helpful because it allows us to empathize with and soothe others.

The most obvious example I have of this is when I am around horses or the ocean. Have you ever just stood by a horse? Pet it? If it is calm, I can feel this powerful calmness in my body as well, like being by the ocean. For this same reason, I never attended a grief group; it didn't make sense to me to go sit in a room full of sad people and then have my nervous system resonate with their sadness. Attending a group where everyone felt what I did felt like an exercise in strengthening my own sadness, not lessening it. I chose to be around people who were not in active grief, who helped me feel more normal and more at ease.

Deep in sleep, one night after Thanksgiving, I had a vivid dream. I was in a house that I didn't recognize, and there were toys scattered about. Standing in the living room with a view of the kitchen, I looked down, and there was an old-fashioned wooden pull toy, the kind that had a little rope and rolled along as a child might pull it. I picked it up, and etched in the wood was an inscription: "SJ ONLY." I thought to myself, *What on earth does that mean?* I woke up still seeing the image, knowing it had meaning but not sure what it was trying to tell me. I mentally rolled over the two letters, SJ, SJ, but they didn't click with anything familiar. I filed it away as noteworthy, but not sure why.

After just two weeks, I returned to the chair. I couldn't sit at home anymore in my lonely emptiness that grew and shrank on a daily basis but consistently felt shades of shitty and shittier. As a therapist, going back to work after losing a child is done differently than, say, going back to computer programming, which was Mark's full-time work. Ethically, it is recommended that we take time off until we can sit with others again in a therapeutic way. Having my own pain, profound suffering made other peoples' suffering insignificant for a while. Despite that, I decided to start seeing clients again rather quickly.

In hindsight, maybe that was a bit soon, but, at the time, sitting around my house with my Shelby, grieving day in and out, was intolerable, like if I waited too long, I might get swallowed whole by the vacuum of grief and never return to work. I had to find a rhythm to my life again.

In the immediate wake of her death, friends and family flocked to our sides. But after that immediate outpouring of support, the world moved on, and suddenly, I was really alone in my thoughts and sadness. People knew my experience, but their lives moved on in a way that mine just couldn't. Working, focusing on other people's problems, took the attention off the awful, heavy emptiness that permeated my cells and belly and moved my awareness to something that felt meaningful. In fact, we actually get a hit of dopamine from acts of service, so going back to doing therapy helped me feel better, even if for brief moments during the day. Movement like dancing also gives us hits of dopamine and serotonin, the feel-good neurotransmitters.

When I am sitting with people, I am sitting with survivors, and I have a mountain of hope for them. I also feel oddly detached from the outcome and believe, as adults, we are all responsible for our own lives. As a result, I trust my only job is to sit and be present with a person in a session; my presence is all I have control over. That focus on my own presence was a mindfulness practice that propelled me out of my own grief. I could not sit in hope for my clients and grieve for myself simultaneously; they activate different parts of the nervous system. Love, hope, joy, peace are ventral vagal states regulating emotional states. Grief is not. In fact, the most significant predictor of outcome in therapy is the quality of the relationship, not the approach or strategy. The quality of the relationship is affected by my ability to attune to clients through my presence.

Monitoring and managing my presence in relationship with clients is all I do, really, paying attention to my whole body, sensation, breathing, and heart, maintaining calmness while listening to clients. Technically, this relaxed state is "parasympathetic arousal," which is the nervous system's relaxation response. I intentionally create this state in my body, attuning to clients so that they begin to resonate with my presence vs. me, resonating with their more activated state, no matter what they are talking about. This is essential, because it engages a person's ventral vagal parasympathetic branch of the nervous system that regulates our breathing, heart rate, and arousal. We, in fact, need social connection to calm and soothe; calm is contagious, but so is anxiety.

When I went back to work, I had only been sharing office space with my two colleagues for a few months before our daughter's death, so I knew them, but not well. I emailed one of them, Aimee, about my loss, and when I saw her, I told her my owl visit story. Aimee introduced me to the goddess Sophia, whose symbol is the owl. She is known as the goddess of wisdom and joy, a feminine divinity of Jesus Christ. She is a celebration of the feminine, and her wisdom is derived from intuition. Typically, I would have kept my owl story to myself, but for whatever reason, after sharing it with the nurses at the hospital, I started to feel the power of her presence in the story of my grief. When Aimee told me about goddess Sophia and representing Joy, I saw the "SJ" from my dream. The meaning of my dream with the toy inscribed "SJ ONLY" suddenly became clear; my daughter's name revealed itself. Her name was Sophie Joy (SJ)—that I now know for certain. It is not declared somewhere on a birth certificate, because that had to be created at the time of her death, and at that point, her name had not come to me. I felt like naming her at the hospital was imposing a name on a body when the spirit of my daughter was gone, and she was the one with a name—not the certificate, not the body. I wasn't sure she would ever tell me her name, but with patience, she did. Sophie Joy.

The owl became a symbol of my daughter and the greater divine; I have called on the owl many times. I wear her. My midwife who delivered Sophie Joy gave me a pair of owl earrings. In fact, I had this piece of costume jewelry of a very tiny, baby turquoise owl that hangs on a shorter chain inside a chain that holds a larger (momma) owl that was given to me by my great aunt sometime in middle or high school. It was a piece of costume jewelry that I had held on to for over twenty years, and the coincidence and symbolism are not lost on me. I thought, *How odd that my aunt gave me this so many years ago, and I kept it*. And it, in fact, has always told a story that is just now unfolding.

For me, the gift of grief was that it cracked me open to a knowing, intuition, and connectedness to the universe that I was born with. I was born knowing, and then somehow learned to unknow, and through grief learned to know again. I think that can be the gift of crisis, if we allow it, a spiritual transformation that helps us evolve and connect more deeply with others and the universe, an opportunity for more connection that is in alignment with our neurobiology, like a recharging season for our own electric aliveness.

One day back at the office, I took a break and went to my first somatic therapy appointment. I told her about my journey, sobbed hysterically, but also expressed that I felt like it was all moving. She gently reflected my words. I could feel her calm presence and knew that I was just in the grief process, and it wasn't going to overwhelm her; she could hold a serene presence while I couldn't. Sitting with her felt like being by the ocean; her nervous system was calm and regulated, even while mine was not. During that session, she said, "Do you mind if we move to the floor?" I said no and took my place laying on my back on a yoga mat with my knees bolstered. She said, "I intuitively feel like we should do this," and she gently held her warm hands over my belly. I could feel this swirl of rolling energy swishing, swinging, soaring, and washing over me. It wasn't grief or sadness, just movement. We sat in this way for a while until it felt done. She completed the session, and I saw her one time after that, and that was the entirety of my therapy about SJ, but I continued to move my grief daily in other ways.

I had danced my way through my entire pregnancy. I taught a class less than a week before Sophie was born. We had a thriving Nia community, so my pregnancy was very public in a way that felt beyond the normal publicness of pregnancy. That would not usually be an issue, really, except when something like this happens. All of a sudden, an event that feels so private is basically out in the community—everyone knows. It felt weird to have my child's life and her story so "out there," a very vulnerable feeling. The first time I returned to the studio was for a holiday celebration, and moments before I entered, I wasn't sure I could "face" the dance floor. I got to the studio door and paused, contemplating leaving, knowing a tsunami of feelings waited on the other side. I opened the door and walked in. Woosh!

Walking into the space felt like another layer of grief. The last time I saw most of these women, I was pregnant, and now I wasn't. I wanted to run, but I didn't; I stepped in, trusting that, in the discomfort, there would come a new ability to keep living, moving in and on, at the same time. I was received by generous hugs and tears, many of us cried together, and even though now I don't see all those women as often, they lifted my heart through that time.

As I returned to teaching Nia classes, I found it was more difficult for me than sitting in the chair. Although clients knew I was pregnant, many didn't ask about my two weeks off or notice that I wasn't pregnant anymore. My clients know me, but they don't know me. My classes were different; they were friends that I had danced with for years. I felt like my Nia friends that had danced with me through my pregnancy knew Sophie Joy as much as I did, really. We had all danced together for nine months, and there is something about dancing together that creates community for me in a unique way.

Another instructor organized a class where each student brought special beads to be placed on a string for me; this simple act held me. In honor of her life, I created a Nia routine called "Mystery" and danced it with students for a few weeks. I actually made the playlist by searching songs that had "mystery" in the title, because I felt like her short life, and life in general, felt like one big unknown, grand design that I was living but couldn't see or feel as a whole. At some point along the many Apple software updates, I have lost countless playlists, and "Mystery" was one of them. When it disappeared, I knew I was done with that part of my grief journey. It served its purpose in helping me move my grief, but then as I evolved and healed, I knew I had to let go of some of the ways I had been grieving.

One of my intuitions that I kept receiving along the way, aside from "write," was to "keep moving." Whether that was breathing, walking, dancing, stretching, talking, traveling, there was this persistent message to keep moving, but that also meant changing the ways that I was grieving. I believe that message to keep moving, whether from a universal power or my body intuition, was essential in resolving the pain and building resiliency. Honestly, I kept dancing, which kept all kinds of emotions flowing, by myself and with others. Grief is like a drop of water in a puddle; when the water drops, it creates ringlets all around. Those ringlets are the grief radiating from our own experience to the community around us, and for a moment, when other people allow themselves to be moved by our grief, they hold it for us for just a second. What a gift that I had such a vast community of ringlets holding my despair, pain, loss, and sorrow, if only for a few minutes or days. Thank you!

Daily, my reckless grieving mind kept wandering aimlessly through the what-ifs. What if I had pushed for the extra ultrasound when I went in for the OB visit the week before she died? What if I had just gone to the ER instead of calling to consult the on-call doctor that Friday? What if I had gone in to check her heart the day before just because? This is a dangerous game the grieving mind plays. The what-ifs of grief are about the mind attempting to gain control of a overwhelmingly powerless experience. It happens in trauma all the time. Still, it is a feeble attempt and does not gain control of the situation. The feeling of powerlessness is overwhelming, so our brain tries to stop the feeling by thinking *what if*, and by answering the question, it gives us the illusion of control for a fleeting second, when really we had none.

Feeling in control is about feeling powerful and safe, the antidote to trauma. I knew that when I was stuck in the what-ifs of grief that any ruminating thought was really attached to a feeling that needed to be processed and felt. Emotions are just sensations in the body waiting to be decoded and acknowledged, and repetitive thoughts clearly indicate that an emotion wants to be recognized. Usually, acknowledging the feeling and feeling the feeling versus playing the cognitive what-if roulette is more healing.

Believe me when I say, though, that any time I dwell on the what-ifs and don't check them right away, the guilt becomes almost unbearable, like a slow-motion steam roller moving over my chest, about to squish me at any moment. I allow myself to feel that guilt in bits and pieces, not all at once, which is another crucial element to healing grief. Sometimes the feelings are so strong and challenging that we can't possibly give them all the space they need in one sitting; it requires taking bite-size pieces day in and out over time, and eventually, the entire tray of grief cake gets digested. No matter what the reason, losing a child is just not the order of things as they should be. She has gone through a developmental stage ahead of me, and that feels all twisted and wrong. I don't think that feeling will ever change, but it has a home in my body, and it drives me to tell our story.

To make sense of what had happened and find justice, I talked to a lawyer about malpractice. There was malpractice, but there is a difference between malpractice, proving malpractice, and paying for losses. The doctors were at fault, but then there is the task of proving fault and putting a price tag on an unborn life, which is an impossible task. Insurance companies will tell you her life was worth between $50k and $100k, because the way they determine "loss" is usually by how much the person earned, and a child has not demonstrated any earning potential. In lawsuit terms, that ain't much. So, we got a lawyer and summoned all the documents. We had an expert witness, an MD, who reviewed the case and would give testimony that the doctors missed a few key things, including the low PAPP-A hormone level and that I was small for gestation.

When we went to see a specialist after we got the results from Sophie's birth about having children again, he told us that he held a special training at the hospital to review the statistical implications for negative outcomes in pregnancy when the hormone PAPP-A is only .1 of 1 percent (that was my level) in a twenty-week pregnancy. At the time, PAPP-A was measured in conjunction with other variables to predict risks for different trisomy conditions, which can be fatal to a baby. So, when our baby did not have the physical mutations associated with a trisomy and was perfectly normal at twenty weeks, that test result was filed away and forgotten, even though levels that low in pregnancy predict issues with the placenta and stillbirth, which was ultimately the cause of her death. The placenta had fibrin all throughout that clogged the flow of nutrients to Sophie Joy. That part was not preventable, but had they been monitoring more closely, they could have caught that she was tiny and stressed, and she could have been born early.

We met with the lawyer a few times and discussed what it would be like to be deposed. I would be questioned about everything, and basically anything in my life was open for discussion, because the lawyer's job for the insurance company would be to create enough doubt about me as a pregnant person that it would be difficult to determine the cause of death—like maybe it was my fault. At the time, the idea of being questioned about my entire life history sounded traumatic. In the end, our lawyer recommended that we not pursue the lawsuit, because although we had a case, by the time we won and paid the experts, the payout from the insurance company for malpractice would barely cover everyone's fees. So, I think I was saved in some ways, because I don't think going through the legal process would have brought me anything at all, except more stress and maybe some money, but at what cost? I've thought about writing a letter to my practitioner at the time, but I think everyone knows their role in how this all happened, and I hope that after my experience, other women are protected from the same tragedy.

When I thought about having kids, I thought about the kids that I would have with me here, not the children that I was going to lose along the way. A friend once told me that motherhood was learning to live with your heart outside of your body. Not only is your heart outside of your body, but by opening up the possibility of bringing in tremendous joy through children, we are also opening up the possibility for tremendous pain through grief and loss. I am here referring to death, but after my experience, I began to realize that there are all types of grief that we open ourselves up to in parenting that can occur not just in death but when our children are born with severe disabilities, get sick, injuries, addictions, grow up and leave home, etc.

This leads me to the questions that haunted me in my grief recovery: 1. Do you have any children? 2. Do you want children? 3. How many children do you have? These seemingly innocuous questions always made me cringe. When asked, "Do you have children?" Or "How many children do you have?" I have to pause for a minute and gather myself. Internally, I reflect. I imagine what they are asking is "Do you have living children?" which is not the same question as "Do you have children?" Then I answer no. But when you ask a person, "Do you have children?" you are actually asking about all of their children—living, cut off from family, given up for adoption, ill, deceased, never born, or adoption that did not work out (perhaps I am missing a few). I generally answer no, because I assume most don't actually want to know about my baby that died at thirty-three weeks gestation or the numerous miscarriages that I had trying to have children. Or what about the couple that perhaps had an only child that died as an adult many years ago? How do they answer? It puts us in a quandary: Do we deny the existence of our deceased children for the sake of ease of conversation, or do we acknowledge their lives, even if they were brief, and sit through all the discomfort because, well, someone asked? I still don't know the answer.

The next question for many women in (assumed) childbearing pre-family years, "Do you want children?" is equally as tricky. Just because someone does not have a living child, as far as you know, does not mean they have not tried to conceive a child, conceived a child, are carrying a child, or have birthed a living baby. The absence of a physical child does not beg the question, "Do you want children?" The truthful answer may be along the lines of "Yes, in fact, I've had a few losses," or "Yes I do, but I am not able to, and it is excruciating for me," or "Yes, but I had to give my child up for adoption," or "No, and every time I am asked that question it makes me feel bad about my choice." I, myself, try to avoid these types of questions with other people after having been through what I've been through, but honestly, before all of our loss, I am sure I asked someone, "Do you wanna have kids?" I like to think that when I know better, I try to do better.

The following summer, Mark and I traveled to Wisconsin to compete in a plein air event. During a pre-show event with collectors, I sat down next to a woman that I knew had bought one of Mark's paintings the year before. We began chatting, and I sensed she didn't truly want to talk to me, so she said something offhand like, "Oh, it must be nice to travel around the country with your husband, no children, no responsibilities," in a punishing tone. I had endured many awkward conversations over the year, but I couldn't swallow the words this time. I looked her in the eyes and said, "I have a daughter, and she died."

The woman froze, looked horrified, and then exhaled, "Oh, well, that's just awful," clutching her handbag tighter in her lap and looking downward to the other side of her body. I walked away. It is the only time I have intentionally shared my daughter's death to lash out at someone's ignorance. Sometimes when we make assumptions, it taps into unknown wounds in others. I try to check all my assumptions at the door these days.

I think we all have our chosen way of moving trauma, and discovering our own intuitive way of moving it is the path to healing from trauma and grief. I kept moving. I did not allow the grief to keep me frozen for too long. When a traumatic event occurs, something that is hyperarousing to our nervous system, our bodies can stay stuck in flight/fight or freeze. When I had overwhelming feelings—panic, sadness, emptiness, hopelessness—I kept moving. I let the roll happen. I never tried to control it, only use the energy to help it flow. Movement in the body—stretching, free dance—helped a lot in moving the emotions. I kept engaging my fight/flight response, even when it felt impossible.

Depending on what we have been through in life, our amounts of unhealed trauma in the body affect our ability to heal and move profound grief, because grief is trauma. Aside from just the hard knocks of life, when we have experienced emotional abuse or neglect in childhood, it is exponentially more challenging to deal with adversity in adulthood. Our nervous systems were literally abandoned by caregivers when we needed connection most. We were left to manage our big feelings on our own before we had the neurobiology to do it. Lacking a mature enough nervous system to regulate our emotions, just like the babies left in cribs, we create coping strategies to make the feelings go away, but this is different than resolving them. If this happens repeatedly, our bodies and minds move us to adulthood, but our capability to feel and resolve feelings stays developmentally young, and our ability to soothe through social connection may not fully develop. When we haven't learned how to ride that intense wave of emotion to the shore and allow it to retreat all on its own, when those big feelings get awakened in adult relationships, our nervous system responds just like the baby or child that is left to cry on its own—scared, overwhelmed, and frozen.

Like a muscle that grows stronger with repeated use, so does our nervous system develop and wire to help us manage feelings—if we have been shown the way. If not, our nervous system has not learned the rhythm of the ride, many feelings become overwhelming, and when they get too intense, we check out through whatever strategies we have learned. From my perspective, I think, I guess luckily, I'm wounded by grief from recent losses, not haunted by all the trauma of my life. Hopefully, all my own work has resolved most of that. Only time will tell.

I had a supervisor once say that the body is a map of the unconscious. The body holds our emotional experiences and has a memory, just like our minds. In some ways, I think that my training in body-based psychotherapy was a stepping stone to helping me face my own grief. Other cultures know that music, movement, and community heal; that is why there are ceremonies involving these elements postwar or other significant events. And although those things worked for me and may work for others, I think the critical factor is finding your own way to move the grief, to find your own rhythm. When grief gets stuck in the body, it becomes difficult to heal, and the original pain resurfaces daily, which can be intolerable.

Quite honestly, sensing and feeling my way through grief was not linear. It gets better, and it gets worse, to this day. But what was clear for me was that feeling my way through versus thinking my way through was the only relief. We do that a lot in our culture—think our way through things, think ourselves out of or into feelings, think our way into jobs, problem-solve our lives—and the art of intuition, which requires being in touch with our bodies and sensation as a way of responding to the world, is lost. A monk once said if you travel everywhere in shoes, then the earth will always feel like leather. We as a culture spend a lot of time in leather shoes.

13

The Gallery, Meaning Making, And Trying Again

Burlington, Vermont: 2011-2013

My private practice quickly filled up again, keeping me busy along with teaching fitness. One afternoon, my colleagues and I were looking for new office space in a building downtown that happened to be for sale, owned by the spouse of an old supervisor. Entering what I imagined to be a charming 1800s brick building, the main room had a retail space with track lighting, and two smaller rooms connected in the back, quaint and small. Nonetheless, it showed promise, even though it had low ceilings. Standing in the space, I could see it as a studio gallery, homey and cozy.

Over the last few years, I heard from other gallery owners that this market was unkind to art galleries, so it seemed unimaginable to open a one artist retail space. I kind of loved this narrative, because it fueled me. It is funny how either encouragement like "You can do it" or discouragement like "You can't do it!" can have the same effect sometimes. I imagine it has something to do with activating a "fight" response. Ha!

From years of selling artwork and running the numbers, it was always clear that, to make it as a successful artist, Mark would have to own his talent and sell some work directly. The next right branding step was brick and mortar, even though many collectors were not local. Funny, right? But somehow, having a physical location seemed essential to continue expanding. After seeing the space, I rushed home and pitched it to Mark. He kind of looked at me in disbelief, so I pushed, and he said, "Okay."

Against most odds, we opened Mark Boedges Fine Art Gallery on Battery Street in Burlington, VT, almost a year to the day after Sophie was born, with only a few months of operating expenses in the bank. A friend at the time made a joke that we should have named it Rebecca's Husband's Gallery because of all the work I put in behind the scenes. Mark and I were both still working full-time at other professions, but we each decided to eke out some retail hours. I invited some dear friends over to create a ceremony to set the intention for our new space, manifest success, and visualize growth and ease.

Late that November, opening night was packed. We got a little press and had a few sales; it felt like another "yes" from the universe. Opening November 21st, 2011 felt momentous; living our lives fully and under our own terms was the best way to make meaning out of our loss. In honor of Sophie, we took one step closer to becoming fully self-employed and Mark becoming a full-time artist. Her short life was the catalyst for us living ours more freely and with less fear.

For as long as I could remember, I had a persistent worry about not having enough money, and after she died, that just went away. Deciding that I had lived through one of the worst things that I could imagine somehow gave me the ability to let go of fears of things that felt less significant. If I could survive losing a child, I could survive going bankrupt, giving our dreams a chance to flower. In the end, I would rather try and fail than regret not ever trying.

At the same time, it gave the tragedy of her death meaning in our lives, which can be a vital part of the healing process. I sometimes wonder what made us capable of moving in a direction that created more meaning in our lives. In a way, I'm not even sure I felt like I was driving the dream. It felt more like we were Hansel and Gretel picking up each piece of bread on our path until we arrived where we needed to be. Luckily for us, it wasn't the witch's house of goodies this time.

When we finally opened the gallery, from the outside, I imagine it seemed like we were just starting, but Mark and I had been building his art career for at least seven years prior. It took planning, perseverance, faith, hope, time, luck, prayers, fairy dust, and magic. Opening the gallery was just another beginning, really—another small step that created way more work. We traded in all of our free time in hopes that eventually Mark could leave IT for good. Time is all we have, really; it is our most valuable asset. So working for ourselves was about having control over our biggest asset.

Heads down, focused, we worked more than we ever had worked in our lives. There were not enough hours in any day, week, month, or year to get everything done, but the promise of the future was worth it. Sometimes I'd wonder if it would just be easier to go back to working for someone else; the security of a regular paycheck and benefits were alluring at times. After losing our daughter, I started to feel like that security was more of an illusion than a reality, though. I could lose a job, get sick, die, all while having a consistent paycheck from someone else. The exchange always felt too great that I trade my creativity, ingenuity, independence, autonomy for a regular salary. We all have our deal-breakers, and I guess that was mine. Mark, too.

The first year the gallery was open, sales ebbed and flowed. Some months Mark would sell a few paintings, others none. Some weeks not a single person walked through the door, and I would zone into Netflix to pass those dry retail hours. Early the following year, Mark won a prestigious award at the Salmagundi Club in New York City—one more award pushing him to keep going.

I'm not sure we ever *decided* to try for kids again that first year, but after a while, I felt like bringing a baby home would be a salient part of our lives. This is when I actually started writing this book—December 30th, 2011: Nineteen days past ovulation (DPO). After a year of not conceiving naturally post–Sophie's birth, we went to Reproductive Endocrinology. They agreed to let us try IUI, even though we didn't technically meet the criteria of infertility. As my story began, that pregnancy took and ended with another miscarriage, and I had to stop writing, because I felt like I might forever be writing about loss. At that moment of giving up, our luck changed.

My bestie and I declared that summer 2012 would be the Summer of Fun and bought matching Mini Coopers. She had just gone through a long-term relationship breakup, and I was over having kids, so we blew it out. We basically just did whatever, whenever—sometimes skipped work, traveled, went to parties—in the name of "fun." Mark and I attended plein air events that summer, sold our tiny 1950s ranch home by the noisy airport, and focused on daily life. A new beginning.

Days grew shorter, leaves began their rainbow symphony, and we moved to a new neighborhood. I can't say I was sad to leave that house that birthed so many grief memories for us. Our new home was in a quiet area with fantastic neighbors.

I went to see my naturopath that fall and reviewed my symptoms around pregnancies. She said, "Sounds like you have a short cycle. Try this herb; it is commonly used to regulate the cycle." I started taking it in October, and in November, we had a positive pregnancy test. After over a year of trying and one failed IUI, one herb did the trick. Truth be told, since it was just a positive test, I thought, *Eh, well, I'm not going to even call the doctor until after six to eight weeks, and I can't possibly go back to the practice we used for Sophie Joy.*

Because of my age and loss, I was now considered high risk and had to see a maternal-fetal medicine doctor. I chose to go to a different hospital, a new scene, an hour away. The idea of going back into the hospital where we birthed Sophie made me sick to my stomach; the smells, the hospital layout, the parking garage—all of it felt too close to our tragedy. I didn't want to relive the grief, conscious or not, every time I had a doctor's visit.

Trauma is about emotional tolerance levels. When an experience is beyond our threshold and is overwhelming (this is different for everyone), we can end up traumatized. The experience may be something that happened directly to us or not. The nervous system does not distinguish between what is happening now in the present moment and what has happened in the past or told to us by a friend. So, remembering or imagining events can be traumatizing. It is also why guided imagery is so helpful; the nervous system knows no time. Close your eyes right now and picture the sound of the waves, the smell of the ocean, the feeling of sand on your feet and the sun on your face; your nervous system begins to respond as if you are actually on the beach, and you can feel it.

When we are emotionally beyond our window of tolerance, we escape somehow through things like dissociation, feeling out of body, drinking, overeating, watching too much Netflix, etc. In response to an actual life threat, whether violence or an accident, we have four options: fight, flight, freeze, or faint. Fight and flight involve our sympathetic nervous system, while freeze and faint involve the dorsal vagal branch of the parasympathetic nervous system. Even without an actual "big event," an experience that triggers overwhelming feelings like fear, shame, guilt, grief, or powerlessness can be activated and push us beyond our ability to cope. In response, our nervous systems can disconnect the thinking part of our brain, and our body goes into fight/flight/freeze/faint. We call it "emotional hijacking," where the prefrontal cortex, the thinking part of our brain, goes offline, and the emotional aspect of our brain drives us. This can happen during an actual event, like losing a child, or when the memory of an event is brought into the present moment, in or out of our awareness.

In these events, like losing a baby, experiencing war, abuse, or anything in between, our perception of the event matters most, not what actually happened. Did we view it as traumatic? If yes, then we imprint a lot of relevant details about the experience, so we are prepared to detect a similar threat in the future. Just a hint of one of the details surrounding the event may remind our bodies what happened, and our alarm system sounds—all out of awareness. This process is designed to help us predict and avoid the threat in the future. Those details get imprinted on our emotional memory centers and our bodies. So, for instance, simply returning to the parking garage at the hospital where I delivered Sophie, I start to get shaky and develop a rapid heart rate. My body is responding to the original trauma of the loss of Sophie simply by the sight and smell of the parking garage. Those sensations are the body memory, somatic memory, of driving in before I was going to deliver, and the overwhelming sadness and grief that accompanied it. If I was not aware of this process, I might start to try to make sense of my heart racing based on what was happening at the moment, like the new doctor, the subsequent pregnancy, or just finding a parking spot. I have to remind myself consciously that what I am feeling in my body belongs in the past, and at this moment, I am safe. Doing this helps calm my body. If I didn't do this, my traumatic experience might escalate.

Trauma is like a snowball. There may be an event or series of experiences that become associated with stimuli surrounding those events. Then each time we experience a stimulus related to the event, like the parking garage, our body memory returns to the original state of arousal. The tricky part is that new stimuli get wrapped up in that arousal if you are not aware that that is what is happening.

So, for instance, I return to the parking garage, start to feel panicky, and I can't find a parking spot. Suppose I'm not aware of what is happening, and I don't consciously attempt to calm my nervous system. In that case, new stimuli get wrapped up in this feeling, so now, not finding a parking spot becomes associated with the feeling of losing Sophie Joy. A week later, I might be looking for a parking spot at the grocery store and then start to feel panicky, but I'm not sure why, and now my original feelings of losing Sophie are attaching themselves to finding a parking spot. Over time, so much of my experience can start to be connected to arousal associated with the trauma of the loss of a baby, so much so that I am living the awful feelings and sensations daily, triggered by something as benign as a cereal box. A significant part of healing from trauma is not letting the body unconsciously associate new memories with the old pain. I was able to do this day in and out; unraveling this snowball is also part of healing from trauma.

Making it through six weeks, I finally dared to call the new doctor's office, and they put me in for the following week. I went to the first visit, and the ultrasound confirmed that I was pregnant with a baby with a heartbeat. During that first visit, I went through my entire history infused with pessimism, and this new doctor listened with teary eyes. She was warm and reassuring and said, "I have seen women with more loss go on to have children."

Hope—there she is again. I was scared to reach for her; numbness and ambivalence felt easier than hoping we might bring home a baby this time. Even though the Lovenox shots were controversial and promised nothing, I begged to be on them again, because it felt like one little thing that I might do to have a successful pregnancy. The doctor agreed, and we scheduled a visit for a few weeks out. After that, there was nothing more to do except wait, hope, and let the next few weeks unfold as they were destined to.

The time between the initial visit, around six weeks and about eighteen weeks, is gone from my memory. I cannot pull one detail from that space in time between meeting our new doctors and the week before our anatomy scan. This amnesia usually happens when something is traumatic; we block it out. It's kind of interesting to me that a span of time where, in some sense, nothing was happening, per se, except me waiting, could have been traumatic, but it was—each day filled with fear and hope at the same time. I know I danced and worked, helped out in the gallery, but no imagery, no distinct moments rise out of that time.

One night, around eighteen weeks pregnant, I had a dream. Mark and I were walking in the dark, gray mist on a beach, almost as if we were walking through dense fog at night. We were barefoot on sand and could hear the ocean or cosmic soup to our left, but it was too viscous to see anything except the stretch of sand before us. Mark was closest to the mysterious cloud, and in between Mark and I was a young child holding both of our hands. The child had these wispy, dirty blond curls, and after a minute, they left us and disappeared into the murky, oceany soup. Mark and I continued to walk along the beach side-by-side. The amount of time we walked alone seemed small in relation to the coastline extending indefinitely in each direction. And then, suddenly, out of the mist, the same child with wispy curls walked out of the soup and grabbed our hands again in between us, and I said with excitement and relief, "You made it, you made it!" And we continued down the beach together. Then, I woke up and had a deep knowing that this little nugget was here to stay for a while; it was soothing and yet not enough to quench all my thirsty fears.

The dreaded twenty-week anatomy scan and bloodwork visit came. Up until now, everything was normal, and doctors were confident that this pregnancy could progress without complication, but in my heart, I felt like we were in for the same ride as our first daughter. We went in for the scan and discovered that we were having a baby girl. She looked and measured normally, but there was one concern. Because the PAPP-A was so low in our last pregnancy, even though that hormone was no longer tested to determine risk for trisomy (testing procedures change rapidly with developing science in the prenatal world), we tested it anyway. As I had imagined, the PAPP-A result was so low that it was undetectable, the same issue that we had with Sophie. PAPP-A is the hormone produced by a functioning placenta, so at around twenty weeks, it was evident that we were in a very similar situation to our previous pregnancy. The placenta was not functioning well, which meant either early delivery or potential stillbirth. There was no chance of a full-term pregnancy. Fuck!

Hearing that news, I had this internal *Ugh, I told you, so* reaction. I had a feeling that whatever had happened last time may have a chance of happening again. Damn Hope! Betrayal! How could I hold on to her anymore? I could barely turn toward her to look her in the face, and yet how could this baby survive if I couldn't find the will to hope now? Parenting lesson one thousand: Our babies call us to be bigger than we are, stretch beyond who we think we can be, and become who they need us to be every day. Deep breath. I thought, *Okay, we were in a similar situation, but our previous pregnancy went to thirty-three weeks, and she was over three pounds at delivery, well beyond viability outside the womb.* Had we known, we could have saved her, and now we know, so we can save her. Everyone in the room knew this baby girl would be born early, but how early? No one had the answer.

We left the visit soggy with sadness and despair. I went home and sobbed and cried and sobbed and cried, threw a good ole fashion tantrum. Why me?! Why her?! Why, why, why? This early in pregnancy, there was absolutely nothing to do but wait and see what happens. Although she measured fine and her anatomy looked good, babies don't usually show growth restriction until twenty-two to twenty-four weeks gestation at the earliest. So, she wouldn't be able to survive outside the womb until twenty-three weeks or more, and even then, if she was born between twenty-three to twenty-five weeks, it would be pushing the limits of medical capabilities.

I started searching, searching for stories of hope. Every morning, I began my day by reading inspirational stories from mommy blogs about their healthy preemie stories. I researched issues specifically related to PAPP-A, fibrin in the placenta. I found many women with recurrent stillbirth, so I decided to only focus on success stories. When I ran out of inspirational preemie blog stories, I started re-reading the same ones, and I vowed to myself that one day I would return the favor. I only allowed stories of hope into our cells, breathing life more and more fully into our baby girl and me. Maintaining hope for her felt like my full-time job now. I was hoping for survival and that she would be born late enough to be healthy.

Four weeks of waiting dragged on, one nanosecond at a time. Twenty-four weeks arrived, and we had an ultrasound scheduled. During the drive to the hospital, I asked the universe for a sign, any sign. This may not seem like a big deal, but after that request, I opened my Facebook app (don't worry, Mark was driving), and the first picture in my feed was a photo of a great horned owl. There she was. I don't even remember why or what the post was about, but I joyfully showed it to Mark and said, "I think it is going to be okay, no matter what."

We arrived at the OB office for our measurement scan to find out how this baby was growing. They began measuring her head, her spine, her femurs while I held my breath. The results showed that our baby girl was in the fifteenth percentile for size—so tiny. The tenth percentile is technically diagnosed as intrauterine growth restriction (IUGR), which our first daughter had. They did not let on how severe the situation was at the time, but they confirmed that she would be delivered early and that the odds were best for her survival without disabilities if she made it to twenty-eight weeks in utero. At that point, survival rate for tiny babies is over 80 percent, and the risk of developmental delays and other issues is less than twenty percent.

In contrast, the survival rate for a twenty-four-weeker outside the momma is around 50 percent. When we got the news, I told the doctors about my dream. I wanted everyone in the room and myself to know and believe that our daughter was going to be born alive and well. I could not face another death of a child, and she was already manifesting her existence, so I felt like we all had to believe she was going to be okay.

Sometimes in medicine, I just believe that the outcome is strongly related to our hopes and beliefs. If I could control that one piece, if I could control the narrative for our unborn daughter, that she already told me that she "made it," then I had to start my parenting right then, telling the world that she was going to make it. At the risk of sounding too "crazy," I told my dream to every single doctor and nurse, so they would believe, too.

After hearing the statistics for delivering a twenty-four-week baby, I told them I was not delivering this early. The doctor said, "Okay, then go home, go on bed rest, even though we are not sure it helps, and come back in two weeks." Another prescription to wait. Waiting is doing nothing and a 24/7 cerebral chess game all at the same time.

Wrangling in my careless monkey mind became my full-time job. I went home from that visit and baked her a twenty-four-week birthday cake and celebrated. Even if she had to be born today, she "made it." So, is this baby girl actually Sophie Joy? I don't know, but my dream was clear; they came from the same cosmic soup. Perhaps we all do.

A few days into bed rest, I declared Ella Sophia as her name. The naming process was so different this time. I was lying in bed, and it just came to me, her name, so I marched downstairs and told Mark we are naming her and "calling her in." I remembered this story from a student's funeral, a woman who danced with cancer and was a midwife for many years. The momma who told the story at her wake recalled one of her children's births, and Laura had been the midwife. The baby was born blue and not breathing, and Laura shouted to the husband something like, "Call his name, you must call him in." So her husband started shouting the child's name, and after a few moments, the child began breathing. I decided I would give Ella her name early so we could call her in. We were going to call her by name so that she knew we were waiting for her, giving her strength to make it to this plane of existence. I texted my family and told them, and I think my dad posted it on Facebook before most people even knew I was pregnant!

Being told to go to bed and stay there indefinitely until this pregnancy was over was excruciating, even armed with a professional level of emotional resourcing skills. At twenty-four weeks, when we knew we would not deliver Ella that early, I went home and went to bed. I had to quit teaching Nia and close my practice. At first, bedrest was kind of fun. I hated stopping everything, but I thought, *Okay, time to catch up on some shows.* Oddly, I obsessively watched *Sons of Anarchy* and *Game of Thrones*, both particularly violent and dramatic, but they kept my focus on something other than my own fears. My good friend from college had a sister who had preemie twins, and another good friend from college had had a preemie herself, so I started calling on those stories of hope to give me strength, because all of their babies were home and healthy. Knowing other people had done this same journey helped me believe that I could, too.

I drank tons of water, ate a lot of protein, rested, and kick-counted like my life depended on it. I would lay down and count ten kicks within two hours. Less than that, and I would need to see the doctor. She had no choice but to come out strong and ready. I told her that she was wanted and that we were going to do these next few months of hard work together. I spent time meditating about nutrients flowing to her and about her growing. Did any of this help? I have no idea, but it was all I had—the power of my intention, focused attention, and will.

I feel like all my training in body-based psychotherapy and messages from the divine had prepared me for this work. I had the tools I needed to stay focused. I told myself repeatedly that my fear was not helpful to our baby spiritually, neurologically, or nutritionally. My job in being her momma was filling my body with feel-good endorphins created by hope, peace, and relaxation. My fear was about me, but this journey was about her, and I had to step it up. I could not succumb to my anxiety. I had to fight, and quite frankly, some days, I got so sick of managing my feelings, I just wanted to drink a bottle of vodka so that I could forget at least for a minute the journey that was ahead. This ability to achieve a relaxed state amid chaos is impossible, and it is my only job now during my work and pregnancy.

We went in for an ultrasound at twenty-six weeks, and Ella's growth was continuing to slow. She was over a pound, but she had fallen to the tenth percentile for growth. Our situation looked more dire. The doctors recommended bed rest in the hospital from now until delivery to get daily ultrasounds, check blood flow to the placenta, and continually monitor Ella's stress level. I just got moved from bed rest to bed rest on steroids. I had never been in a hospital overnight as a patient before, and now I was here to stay for a while. I didn't go home from that visit; I went over to Labor and Delivery.

I was checked into a room all by myself. In some ways, I felt relief, like I had gotten us this far, and now doctors were helping with the rest of the pregnancy. I didn't have to make any more decisions on my own. Mark left, and I settled in. I had my phone and computer and a stack of books. He had to go to work and keep the gallery open, so I was on my own most of the time. I quickly found a routine in this new home.

I would wake up in the morning, read, meditate using a track that altered brain waves, get wheeled down for an ultrasound, get to see Ella on screen, and then hold my breath until a doctor came in during rounds to tell me that the results looked okay. The ways that they have of detecting a baby's stress are good but not great. I would then get hooked up for hours to a monitor where they take this round device, search for Ella's heart, and then harness the monitor to my belly with bungee-like straps to hold it in place. Within seconds, Ella would kick the monitor repeatedly, swim around to get out from under it, and proceed to hide. The nurse would come back in and reset the equipment, hoping to get twenty minutes of "tape." I guess the twenty minutes of heart rate printed out was statistically enough to show that Ella was doing okay and that her heart rate wasn't consistently dropping, which would indicate that she was under duress and needed to be delivered.

The monitor's sound is still traumatizing to me, even though I made them turn it to the lowest volume every time I was hooked up to the machine. It is a spacey pulse that sounds like Darth Vader breathing quickly while cupping his hands over his mouth, closing and opening them repetitively. Then all of a sudden, because Ella would move and kick the monitor off, the sound would drift off and stop, and the chart on the printout would flatline for a while. Then the twenty minutes would start all over again.

I would spend hours a day hooked up to that machine, trying to get twenty minutes of tape, then if something looked a little off, I would be "NPO," which is code for "no food or drink" in case surgery is needed. These were my days in the hospital on bed rest. That was my work at that time, just keeping myself mentally capable of sitting through the agony of the wait, and the wait felt like life or death for my daughter every moment of every day.

One nurse that stands out in particular was one of my "primaries" at Dartmouth. When you are on bed rest in a hospital, you get a few primary care nurses who work with you when they are on shift. At the time, I was reading Eckhart Tolle's *A New Earth*, because aside from watching *Game of Thrones*, what else do you do when the current moment is intolerable? I was grasping at reading any spiritual book that could give me some relief. After a stillbirth, having another tiny baby inside of me, riding up to the edge of what she could handle in utero was like strolling up to the edge of the Cliffs of Moher, laying on my belly, and peering over down into the sea.

Now, in fact, when I had that option in real life in my travels to Ireland in my early twenties, I did not fucking walk up to the edge! Some people did, but I did not! There are the people who walk up to the rim for fun, and those who think walking up to the edge is scary. I am the latter. Every moment of every day felt like I might lose my balance and go tumbling over, and that maybe we were pushing the pregnancy too far, and Ella might fall back into the ocean soup again. A tug of war between my will and hope versus the omnipotent force of the tides of the universe.

My nurse saw the books that I was reading and started talking to me about Eckhart Tolle. She started telling me about her life and spiritual journey, and I began sharing mine. I felt like she was honestly an angel sent to deliver hope to me while I was on bed rest. As I tentatively shared my story about Sophie Joy and the owl and the dreams, she started to share her experiences.

One day while we were talking, knowing she had worked on a cardiac unit before labor and delivery, I asked her if she had ever had an experience that she could not explain about the afterlife, and she said she had. She told me about a story when a gentleman she was caring for flatlined and was considered dead for a few minutes. She said that he flatlined, and everyone rushed in to begin offering resuscitation. In the few moments of chaos, while he was flatlined, she banged her thigh really hard on a corner of something in the room. After a few minutes of being gone, they were able to bring him back. When he came back to consciousness, he asked the nurse, "How is your leg?" She said she looked at him and did not know what he was talking about. Then he said, "You banged it and said ouch. I saw you do it while I was watching from up in the corner." She said at that moment, she remembered that she had banged her leg really hard during the whole ordeal, and really there was no way he could have "seen" it while he was flatlined.

I was amazed. I had always heard of these stories and read these types of stories, but to hear her tell it firsthand was pretty inspirational. It was the story I needed on that day to get me through. I prayed to whoever was listening; maybe I had spirits in the corners of my room waiting to help. In a way, I felt like I was bargaining. Spiritual stories became my food, and I promised to the universe that, in return, I would share my story on the other side to nourish others. In desperation, we all start making deals with a god/goddess, like if I can have this one thing, I will do whatever in return. In those moments, I would have negotiated almost anything. Sharing my story seemed like a small exchange. After Sophie, I knew I had to write, but now I knew for sure I had to share my story, too. Writing was just the first part.

Amid the monitoring, ultrasounds, the waiting, about a week into bed rest, they told me that they were totally booked and had to put a roommate in with me. I had no choice, really. They pulled up the curtain, and in came a pregnant woman who was also at risk for preterm delivery. She arrived in the late afternoon and had requested pain meds. We were only divided by a curtain. They did not give them to her, so she started crying out in pain for hours, hours, until about 1 a.m. So now, I am thinking, *This was already bad, but now I have a roommate who is pregnant and in opiate withdrawal, so now I am not just in an uncomfortable situation, but my surroundings are relentless.* I made the mistake of offering her the remote because I saw she had nothing, and I had a phone, iPad, etc. The TV was blasting until 2 a.m. when I got the courage to peer around the curtain and saw she was fast asleep. I took that remote and hid it; my generosity was exhausted.

The next morning, she was rolled out for ultrasound, and so was I, but when I came back, two nurses I had not met asked me to sit in a chair by the window. I was wondering what was going on; it all felt very formal and official. I didn't know if this was about my test results or something about my pregnancy or what. They start stripping my bed and bagging my belongings, simultaneously combing through my hair. They told me that my roommate had bed bugs and lice, and now I had to be checked, moved, and all my belongings had to be removed from the campus and heat treated. Ha! WHAT?! *I am really in hell right now, like I did something in a previous life that has left Goddess Sophia so mad at me that I am getting taught a lesson about life and privilege or something.* They take all my stuff except my phone and move me to another room where I am alone for the night. I am laughing and crying simultaneously. Somehow, bed bugs and lice are a nice distraction from my own work.

After a day, another roommate is assigned to share my room. Solitude was short-lived. Thank goddess, she was thoughtful and sweet, and we had a few good talks. She was much further along than I and was only in the hospital for a couple of days. I was so jealous that she could decide whether to stay or go. If I chose to leave the hospital, I could be risking Ella's life.

That evening, I had a new night nurse, and she was chatty with my roommate and me. After a long talk, she shared how she was an old-school nurse and gave all her patients back rubs at night. She said she had worked in the maternity ward for years, and that was her training. My roommate was all excited. I was caught up in the powerlessness of patienthood and, hardly feeling like I could say "no," I reluctantly agreed as well to this nighttime massage routine. I think I've been a therapist too long for something like a nurse doing me a massage favor to feel like a favor. I've heard too much trauma to totally trust that kind of offer. Sad, really. Now, I'm a grown woman and a therapist, and do you know what I did? When she returned to give us our back rubs, I had my iPad still on, but I pretended to be asleep. I fucking hid from her. In that state, I just could not muster a "no" when it was needed.

Little did I know that this feeling of struggling to tell doctors and nurses "no thank you" would be part of my journey every day from there on out. That was the last time I "hid" from the nurses or doctors; I had no choice. Parenting lesson one thousand and one: If we hide as parents, sometimes our children take the blow. It is crucial to know when to hide, run, or fight. Occasionally, we over rely on one strategy, like always running or always hiding, but when we don't have access to all of our responses (fight, flight, freeze, faint), we can be more easily traumatized. Studies show those who flee in the face of fear end up less traumatized in the long run.

That Saturday, ultrasound arrived in my room to scan Ella's blood flow, and the tech thought that the images looked a little concerning. The weekend shift of doctors and nurses are a totally different crew than the weekday staff, so these folks did not know my whole story; they were just following the orders left from the weekly doctors. The resident working for the weekend took a look at the ultrasound blood flow results and said that she saw some "reverse flow," which basically meant Ella had to be delivered immediately. Reverse flow indicates the blood from the artery that brings nutrients from the placenta to the baby has stopped delivering blood, and actually, the blood has begun to reverse flow from the fetus. Not good at all. I started sobbing. *I may deliver Ella before twenty-eight weeks, and twenty-eight weeks is the golden statistic. No, no, no, no, no, I will not accept this. This is not what is happening.* I was full-on ugly crying, calling Mark, and my roommate was checking out. I was so jealous that her little stay was uneventful, and she got to leave. She handed me a note on the way out.

Other doctors started coming in for a consultation, and they decided to call in a doctor who had been working with me. She looked at the results and then called to have another ultrasound technician that the doctor knows and trusts come up and do another analysis. This technician did the second ultrasound and took photos that she delivered to my doctor at home. My second team, the primary team, decided that there was no reverse flow, and that Ella wouldn't be born today. *Exhale.*

I opened the tear-stained note and read a message of hope from my new friend, along with her phone number. I think she felt as bad as I did that she got to leave and was further along in her pregnancy. Kind of like survivor guilt. Motherhood is a sisterhood, and on the delivery floor, we are all wound in a web of birthing and dying. The veil is thin.

This is how most days went for me on bed rest in the hospital. We would start the day gathering information about Ella's status, which generally invited more questions than answers. Each bit of inconclusive data had to be investigated to the fullest to ensure Ella was safe. Unfortunately, like the ultrasounds and stress tests, most exams gave mixed results, and the only way to proceed was to gather more data. After the ultrasounds, I was hooked up to a monitor basically twenty-four-seven until Ella was born.

After the scan scare, I was returned to my old room alone, and they gave me a second dose of steroids for Ella's lungs. They also put in the order to begin a magnesium sulfate treatment. There are a few complications to having early babies, and the inability to breathe because of immature lungs is one of them. Others are brain bleeds and cerebral palsy.

They called in the nurse to come check my IV. I'd had one in for a few days in case I had to be rushed to surgery. The IV wasn't good anymore, so the nurse said she needed to replace it. She was the same one who told me that my roommate had bed bugs the week before. To reduce any additional pain, I asked her to call the IV team, because my veins are hard to get. She assured me she was rock solid at this skill and asked if she could try. I told her that she could try one time, but I needed her to call in the team if she didn't hit it. She agreed, she prepped, we breathed deep, and she missed. She started to dig, and I had to stop her. No more hiding or appeasing. I asked her to call the IV team. They arrived, and one stick and done. IV was in. When someone puts pressure on me, like trying to change my mind, that's when I need the most energy to push back and say no. After almost two weeks of bed rest, hiding was most preferable, but I couldn't hide from the IV.

Shortly after, the nurses explained that I would be administered magnesium sulfate, a compound found in Epsom salt, through IV for twenty-four hours. The drug would help coat Ella's nervous system and reduce her risk of brain bleeds or cerebral palsy. The risk to me if the drug reached toxic levels could be a heart attack or respiratory failure, so I would be checked hourly. Lovely.

Drip in, the procedure began. Quickly, I felt nauseous, hot, floaty, dissociated, like I had a terrible flu. My skin was flushed and itchy, I wanted to get up and move around, but I didn't have the energy to do it. I felt so terrible and high, my worry about Ella faded into a focus on my physical discomfort. I'd traded my pain—a weird, temporary reprieve. I lost track of time, and I couldn't focus on the TV, but I left it on so I could stare at something aside from the vanilla-colored walls imprisoning me. Every hour, day and night, a nurse came in, shook me awake, and asked me a few questions to make sure I was still lucid, then I drifted off again. Finally, we made it through the treatment, and I began to regain awareness.

Within a day, the neonatologist came by to prepare us for delivery. I said, "No one said anything about delivery," and he said, "They only send me in when a baby is about to be delivered," and that is how I found out Ella would be born soon. He discussed with us the common complications and what was going to happen after she was born. She would be taken immediately and intubated until they could determine if she could breathe on her own. There were risks of brain bleeds but less so because she would be close to twenty-eight weeks and the first few hours of her life would be spent in an incubator hooked up to monitors and feeding tubes. I read something by a neonatologist that preemies declare themselves moments after birth. In those first twenty-four to forty-eight hours, the nurses and doctors wait to see how they declare themselves. Some of them are just born fighters, or they have many complications right from the start, which usually determines the course of their NICU stay. As I write this, I am filled with pride that my baby girl is a fighter; she is strong, mighty, and fierce. Do not be misguided by her tiny stature, for her spirit is that of a lioness.

14

Ella

Dartmouth-Hitchcock Medical Center: May 2013

On Monday, I saw my regular doctor and asked her if Ella was going to be born soon. She said, "We are going to keep going until we can't keep going; there is no way to know."

I said, "I had a dream she was born on May 7th." It was May 6th.

We laughed, and she said, "Maybe. I do trust a mother's intuition."

After I had had the treatment of Epsom salts, I had been concerned about her heart rate. Although it was "normal," it was low for Ella. She usually ran kind of high, and at times, instead of beating around the 160s, it was hanging in the 110s, 120s. On May 7th, twenty-eight weeks and one day, her ultrasound was fine, but her stress tests were starting to look funky and unclear.

I began to crack. I was literally right at the cliff's edge, knees shaking, heart racing, trembling with fear, and I did not think I could take one more loop in the roller coaster. I now know that the doctors were likely making very conservative choices with me, but at that time, my only experience was doctors not making the choices that would have kept my first daughter alive.

To gather more information about her status, the doctors recommended giving me Pitocin. Pitocin would start contractions, and if Ella's heart rate dipped, then they would know she was stressed and needed to come out immediately. If not, we could ride along a little further. So, I agreed. We started the procedure.

I could feel the first contraction, even though they said the dose was so low I wouldn't feel it. Sure enough, her heart rate dipped and then went back to normal, then another contraction, and it fell again. I started crying, heart racing, panic pulsing through my nerves. I told them we needed to stop, but they wanted more data before making a decision. I said this was going too far, and I was done. I had taken Ella as far as I could inside of me. We were at twenty-eight weeks and two days; she was going to have to do the rest outside of me. The nurse said okay and showed the doctor the results. I was rushed to the operating room, because Ella was under stress; she had to come out quickly. There was some discussion if we had time for an epidural or if I needed to be knocked out, and the doctor said we had time.

They rushed me into the OR. An anesthesiologist began prepping me and had an epidural in me within moments. From my room to OR and prepped was maybe five minutes. I remember many people in the OR, bright lights. They laid me down, strapped my wrists down, and put up a curtain between me and my lower half. Mark came in, they made an initial incision, and I was numb. They began to cut. Awake and terrified, contemplating my own and perhaps Ella's death felt like being chained down, forced to watch someone drop my child from twelve stories, hoping that the firefighters' bouncy mat was placed just in time. That waiting between the drop and landing was delivery.

Frozen panic iced my body until, all of a sudden, I could hear the warmth of the most angelic voice whispering positive encouragement in my ear while gently stroking my hair. I'll be honest, most anesthesiologists I've met have left me feeling weird, but it was like the magical shift change (there was a shift change right as I was being admitted, people swapping in and out) had left me with this angel of an anesthesiologist, delivered here to coach me through this awful moment. I held on to her voice and sweet nothings—"You are doing great, a few more minutes, keep breathing"—like a baby to a binky. I relaxed into her voice for a few seconds, then I felt this hard jerking in the lower half of my body—no pain but tons of pressure. I felt like I was being pulled apart—the force was unreal. And then I heard what you never want to hear. The resident attempting to deliver Ella stressed, "I can't get her head out."

WTF!? My head was swimming. *Get the JV squad out of my abdomen and bring in the Varsity team NOW!* The doctor jumped on the table. She was maybe five feet tall and kneeled next to me, pulling Ella out. This tiny woman quickly took over the entire mission, and the room got quiet. No cry. In a flicker, Ella was out. A crew of scrubbed doctors swarmed her, shuffling in a huddle to the NICU, and Mark followed. I was left with the doctor's team and my whispering angel, so I homed in on her voice again and closed my eyes. Tears of fear and relief painted my cheeks with a web of uncertainty. Those moments of deafening blackness swallowed me up and sucked the air out of my lungs, squeezed my heart, while the devil stared me in the face, all the while not knowing if Ella was safe. Arms strapped down, staring at a blue sheet, angel in my ear, I waited.

After what seemed an eternity, Mark came back in and said, "She is breathing on her own," and the doctor showed me a picture of the soles of her feet. She was alive. The angel in my ear had won. Ella was here—boldly, profoundly, firmly, willfully—and was breathing on her own. Who does that at one pound twelve ounces and twenty-eight weeks of development? My baby. She does. She slays. She declared herself with the will and strength of an Amazon goddess, and a few days after her birth, when she looked me in the eye from her Isolette, I knew this little soul was here to do some great work. Whenever I fear my own strength, I think about my daughters and the power that they all have had from their moments of conception.

Now, I know that sounds tiny, and it is small, but my heart leapt out of my chest. She was alive, twenty-eight weeks and two days, and well over a pound. Now this felt like something to work with. The wait was over. The next phase, NICU, had begun. She was about the size of a bag of jelly beans. She was born alive, so there was joy, but she could also perish or have a life full of medical complications, so there was fear, power-lessness, guilt, and sadness all wrapped up in one baby burrito.

Even though our first daughter is only with us in spirit, Ella Sophia carries her name to honor her life. And who knows—maybe there is a little Sophie in Ella. Chimera, in genetics, refers to multiple DNA strands in cells. They have found, for example, male DNA in female adult brains, attributed to babies that a mom carried, which then gets integrated into the mothers' body, even in their brain neurons. This also happens with siblings, so any fetuses I carried before Ella have left their DNA in me and may also have shared it with Ella. Sophie's DNA is for-ever in my cells and now potentially passed on to her siblings. Perhaps there are parts of Sophie Joy"s DNA in Ella and me. It is weird to think about, but it actually gives me comfort.

They sewed me up, which took three times the length of delivery, and when finished, they wheeled me back to my room for about thirty minutes to recover. Still in my hospital bed, because the sensation had not returned to my lower half, Mark wheeled me to the NICU to meet Ella.

There is nothing that prepared me for seeing a baby the size of my palm curled up in an incubator. She was perfect. I was scared to see her at first, afraid she might look weird or disproportionate, but nature is an amazing goddess. She creates those little people just perfectly for their journey from early in the womb. I don't think I was ever prepared for how little control I had over helping these babies of mine be whole and healthy. As a mom incubator, I had some control, eating right and tak-ing care of myself, but beyond that, there was not much that I could do; my babies were doing a lot on their own from conception in many ways. In an incubator to maintain body temperature, keep a sterile environ-ment, and monitor heart rate, oxygen levels, feeding, and Continuous Positive Airway Pressure (CPAP), I wasn't allowed to hold her initially. I sat outside that little plastic box, half loopy post-surgery, and just stared at her, like watching fish in an aquarium.

To my surprise, she just looked like a little baby bird with no feathers, the smallest diaper you have ever seen folded like origami to fit her butt, and miniature fingernails the size of flecks of dried oregano.

15 |

Entered NICU As Fighters, Left As Warriors

Dartmouth-Hitchcock Medical Center: May 2013 - July 2013

My bed was rolled up alongside the Isolette. I couldn't touch her, but I knew she knew I was there, so I talked and sang to her, swaddling her with my voice. Prosody, the tone of a caregiver's voice, is a meaningful way that babies regulate their nervous systems. Our hearts put off a magnetic field that extends ten times that of our brains. I imagined that, sitting next to her, even though I couldn't hold this fresh little being, I was still helping her.

I felt so powerless watching this raw baby in a box. I knew she knew my voice, so I kept singing. I told her she would be fine, just like I did when I found out she was tiny at twenty-four weeks gestation. While she was in the womb, I told her repeatedly, "You are strong, you are loved, you are wanted, you will make it." I don't know if I was telling that to her or myself. I think she already knew she was here to stay, and I was the one who needed convincing. Children are funny like that. I believe they come in on their spiritual journey to teach us. The best parenting is done when we can become who our children need us to be. All of my daughters, as well as those little spirit babies that never made it in physical form, have required me to become someone more trusting and open to alternative ways of knowing the world—the kind of knowing that comes from the belly and heart, not what I learned in textbooks.

She was hooked up to an IV (to get antibiotics), a heart rate monitor, a feeding tube through her mouth, and a CPAP forcing air into her nose, and the Isolette had a warmer to help keep her body temperature. She was intubated immediately after birth, but they removed the apparatus to see if she could breathe independently, and she did, no respirator. I hated seeing her all hooked up to machines, but she was clearly a fighter. Ella Bean was here and here to stay. Ella bean, vanilla bean, about the size of a jelly bean.

Relieved pregnancy was over, I had hopes that NICU would be different, easier maybe. In some ways, because there was a team of doctors and nurses now responsible for Ella, not just my body, it felt easier but no less scary in terms of life and death. It was a constant roller coaster; Ella would have symptoms, and the doctors would say, "Well, it could be this totally benign thing that doesn't matter, or this other thing that can be deadly," every day for the first month. Ella was born one pound, twelve ounces, and you can be born that small, but you can't stay that small for any amount of time. She even dropped to one pound nine ounces on the second day!

She was placed in an Isolette on the high-risk side of the NICU, designed for babies with multiple complications, hooked up to monitors sounding warning alarms constantly. I was happy that she was here and alive, but now I had to leave her here, alone in this firework display of bells and whistles, some of which were her own. It felt like abandonment, even though she was surrounded by professionals.

Exhausted and terribly nauseous, I went back to my room to try to get some sleep. Despite my discomfort, pain from surgery, nausea, the nurse arrived to teach me how to pump. She fitted me for the funnels that went over my breasts, trying a few different sizes over my nipples, eyeballing the fit, and then picking one for me. She said, "If you don't fit the funnels correctly, you will end up with cracked, sore nipples and won't get enough milk." Holding the funnels up to my chest, she hit the power button on the machine, and started pumping. This system was only slightly more sophisticated than the apparatus made for milking dairy cows. *Mooo.* The nurse explained that, because Ella was a preemie, my milk supply might not come in that well, so I would have to pump around the clock every three hours to get it to come in. Pumping felt like someone took two vacuum cleaner hoses and placed them on my nipples. It was a new level of *Are you fucking kidding me? This is what I must do now?* But it was what Ella needed.

I was so tired, I could drop, but I just held the pump to my breasts while nurses and doctors wandered in and out, trying to get two to five milliliters of milk. Some moms can pump ten to fifty milliliters after delivering a full-term baby. I pumped for fifteen minutes and got a few drops, so demoralizing. The nurse cheered me on. "That's great!" she exclaimed, but I couldn't get excited about an eye-dropper amount of milk, not even with the nurse cheerleader. I was hell-bent on giving Ella breastmilk, because preemies' stomachs are very immature. If given formula, they have a much higher risk of developing necrotizing enterocolitis (NEC), a deadly infection of the intestine that can kill a baby in hours, even if detected. So, no pressure or anything, but I had to do everything I could to help Ella stay healthy and come home with us. There I was—sick, tired, post old-school C-section, learning how to pump with an audience. Serious good times right there. So it began, around the clock, setting alarms overnight to attempt to pump enough milk for Ella.

Amid the pumping lesson, I told the nurse that I was feeling unusually nauseous and thought maybe it was the pain killers. So sick that Mark went to the NICU without me. I got up and started walking around the room, hoping it would make me feel better. It did temporarily, so I ventured back to the NICU, slowly making my way the few hundred yards to Ella.

I sat down next to her Isolette. She was so tiny and orange, really orange, like an Oompa Loompa from Charlie and the Chocolate Factory. She had jaundice, like all babies that tiny, and after two days of antibiotics, she was going to be put under red lights to help them clear the bilirubin from her bloodstream. The bilirubin is the byproduct of breaking down red blood cells and is usually removed by the liver. Micropreemies typically need help in this process, because their livers cannot clear everything quickly enough. Left untreated, jaundice can cause serious health issues, like cerebral palsy, brain, or organ damage, but this was the least of her health issues at that point.

I began singing and talking to her, since that was all I could do. At some point soon, I might be able to put my hand in and cup her navel orange–sized head. A nurse came by to talk to me about how to touch her, since preemies are very sensitive. They need and want touch, but it must be firm, even though they look so fragile. Delicate touch is over-stimulating for them. Preemies will throw their hands out like a stop sign to tell you to stop doing something they don't like—a talk-to-the-hand gesture.

Sitting in the NICU, I was oscillating between focusing on Ella and then being distracted by my increasing nausea. Finally, it got so bad that I thought I would throw up, so I left again. I kept feeling this struggle of needing to be with her, but also like I was going to vomit at any moment. Walking eased my stomach, so I ventured to the outdoor court-yard to get some fresh air, but I knew there was no avoiding getting sick. Circling the brick patio a few times, I headed back to my room and began projectile vomiting all over the bathroom. I had never been ill like this before in my life. Certain it was the pain killers, I stopped taking everything, but my primary nurse said she believed that I had an ileus (obstructed bowel), apparently a complication due to abdominal surgery. In rushed a whole cleanup crew, so now, I had doctors, nurses, and the cleanup crew crammed in my room, and after changing my clothes—ding, ding, ding—in came the nurse with the pump. Apres fifteen minutes of pumping, I eked out another few milliliters of milk, and exhaustion started taking over.

Meanwhile, all I can imagine was little Ella in that NICU with all those machines all by herself. Heartbreak does not describe the pain.

I was desperate to feel better, because I couldn't help Ella when I couldn't even help myself. I fell asleep for a couple of hours, and upon waking, the nurse gave me a popsicle to try to eat. A few licks in of cherry pop, I was again projectile vomiting all over the room. I was less than twenty-four hours post-surgery, I should've hardly been walking, and I was up walking and puking. In came cleanup crew number two, and I fantasized that they could wash away all my feelings of powerlessness with their bleach and rags.

The doctor finally visited and agreed with the nurse that I likely had an ileus but assured me that she could hear some gut motility, so it wasn't a total blockage. The young resident explained that if it didn't remedy soon that they would treat me by inserting a vacuum tube down to my gut connected to the wall behind my hospital bed. It would vacuum all the air out of my stomach, relieving the blockage. WTF? Can you say, "Hell no"? I was not going through one more invasive procedure. After the doctor left, my loving nurse reassured me that the procedure she explained was a last resort and that it was best to get up and keep walking around because that was the best way to get the gut moving, so back on my feet, off I went.

I walked down to the cafeteria, hung out with my mom, had the loudest, most offensive gas coming out of my body that you can imagine, and under normal circumstances, I would have been so horrified I might have had to move to another country, but I was in so much pain I just did not care. I only wanted to feel better, and if walking and passing gas was the only way to avoid the vacuum suction down my esophagus, well then, I was up to the challenge. I weaved between pumping every three hours, trying to walk enough to begin to feel better, getting cat naps, and squeezing in visits with Ella.

Finally, by the second day, I was no longer vomiting and was given the green light to go home, which, after weeks of being in the hospital, felt so inviting, yet it meant not being down the hall from Ella. Post-surgery on the maternity ward, I was only a little walk away from the NICU, and now I would have to leave the hospital without her. Again,

I was faced with having to go against every motherly instinct in my body to leave my under-two-pound baby in a heated cube in a big room with strangers, this time staying many miles away. The doctors and nurses were angels, but I still had a visceral reaction to leaving my child in the hospital overnight, and this was just the beginning. I would leave her fifty-five more times before I could bring her home with me.

The NICU is not set up for overnight parents unless I wanted to sleep next to the Isolette in a reclining nursing chair in a room full of other Isolettes and preemies with all the sounds that came with it. One night, they offered me a bed on the pediatric wing, but I couldn't sleep there. I literally walked all the way over, they showed me a hospital room with a single bed, I could hear children crying through the door, and I just couldn't do it. I left, thanks but no thanks. I could barely tolerate the sounds of my own sick child, never mind everyone else's.

I spent the rest of the day sitting next to Ella under her sun lamps, talking to her and singing. Her alarms would sound, and I would look over at the nurse, back to her heart rate and breathing monitors, then to the nurse again to see if she was going to come save Ella. The beeping, like the pregnancy heart monitor, became a sound I dreaded. Preemies cannot regulate their heart rate or breathing because of their immature nervous systems.

Research on trauma actually was inspired by this phenomenon in preemies. The vagus nerve controls our fight/flight and relaxation response, but researchers discovered that freeze and faint are activated in a different branch of the nervous system—the dorsal vagal system versus the ventral vagal system, the latter of which, when active, regulates our heart rate and breathing. Essentially the vagus nerve can kill you by slowing down your heart and breathing so much that it stops but is also essential in human connection and interaction, which regulates our breathing and heart rate. Kind of a double-edged sword.

In preemies, the vagus nerve is immature. Therefore, they can drop their heart rates ("destatting") and stop breathing (apnea), slowing their nervous system so much to the point that they can die if not resuscitated. The way a preemie matures their vagus nerve is by learning to bring their heart rate back up on their own, and to start breathing on their own again when they stop.

Sitting next to Ella, I would see her mouth get dusky, her heart rate numbers would drop on the monitor, the alarm would sound, and then we would all wait to see if she could bring her heart rate back up on her own or if she would need some kind of stimulation, like me touching her. Watching this monitor early on, I could not ride it out. I had to touch her to reactivate her nervous system, helping her either to start breathing or to bring her heart rate back up again. It was too much.

For weeks to come, we did this dance. I would watch my itty-bitty baby turn blue in the face from not breathing, and if we all waited too long to stimulate her, she would have had to be "bagged," meaning airbag resuscitated. The level of fight or flight in my body, a sympathetic nervous system response, the entire time leading up to Ella's birth was enough stress to dysregulate a troop of Army Rangers. In fact, at one point, my younger brother, who completed Ranger training, sat in the NICU for one day and said he did not know how I could handle the stress. I had to learn to contain my fear day in and out while I watched Ella struggle to gain the ability to regulate her own nervous system.

By evening, when it was time to go, I sobbed a waterfall of tears and left with Mark. I would be roughly an hour away from her. The silent car ride was heavy. I kept thinking about Ella and what would happen if they didn't stim her soon enough and she had to be resuscitated. Or what if I got a call in the middle of the night because she got NEC and needed emergency surgery. The spiral of worry carried me into dizzy distress.

We got home, and I gave some love to the pets and headed to bed. I couldn't really sleep and had my alarm set to wake me up every three hours to pump. My initial plan was to try to go to sleep at nine to get up at midnight, then three and six. I didn't sleep very well and kept waking up in between the alarms, and after midnight I walked into the spare bathroom and vomited. I panicked because I knew I still had the ileus, and I was supposed to be in the hospital, but I wasn't going back to be hooked up to the vacuum, so I dragged Mark out of bed to go for a walk down the street in the middle of the night.

There we were, around midnight, strolling up and down my quiet road, hoping and willing my gut back to motility. At least that's what I was doing. Mark was probably just hoping to get a few more hours of sleep. My personal prescription for middle-of-the-night walking worked, and I began to feel better. I finally slept for a few hours before getting up to pump, and then went back to sleep for a few hours. I awoke that morning feeling a little refreshed, and we drove back to the hospital.

My heart blew out of my chest when I saw Ella. She was doing okay; every day now was a massive step for her. Although Ella had dropped weight to one pound, nine ounces, which they anticipated because of the IV and antibiotic treatment, she was still breathing with help from a CPAP, no respirator, which was significant. After the antibiotics and sun lamps, I could now hold Ella. I could finally wrap her up in my arms.

The nurse set me up in the big blue nursing chair with pillows under my arms. She opened the Isolette, picked Ella up like a newborn kitten, carefully positioning her on my bare chest inside my shirt, diligent not to disturb one of the half a dozen tubes and wires hanging off her tiny frame. They called this "kangaroo" holding, where I tuck her naked body on mine. Sweet, little Ella, her twiggy legs folded under her in child's pose and her head right on my heart. Namaste, my tiny miracle. Her little noggin was the size of a ripe Florida orange covered in a little hand-knitted cap, donated by people who make hats for preemies. Her color was more red now than orange, but her skin suit was a little loose and baggy, like two sizes too big. She had no time to put on fat in the womb; all the calories she got were going to growing her brain. They call it head sparing. She was perfect, though.

I soaked her in through my skin, and for a few brief moments, her monitors were quiet. Her body was calm and regulated, ventral vagal dominant. We sat still, feeling like the sun had risen for the first time after twenty-nine days of darkness. Kangarooing became my job in the NICU aside from pumping. When little babies are placed skin to skin day after day, they grow faster, stay more regulated with less desatting, and mature more quickly. In 2013, NICUs in other countries were built to allow moms to stay and kangaroo twenty-four seven, but not here, or in most hospitals in the US.

Mice that are licked more often postnatally develop more of a capacity to downregulate stressful situations because of how their epigenetics are affected by maternal nurturing. I know we are not mice, but it makes sense to me that contact with mom and dad during those early days, even if the babies are sick and in NICU, affects their nervous system development. There were babies around Ella withdrawing from opiates, and they would cry and cry. They would give them some opiates to ease withdrawal, but I overheard a neonatologist say that the best treatment for the babies was kangarooing and holding them. Sadly, there were rarely adults in the NICU to hold these babies. I was one of the only caregivers in the NICU every day, but it was only because I had closed my practice. Mark couldn't be there daily because he had to return to work. Putting my practice on hold was a difficult decision that we couldn't afford, but I felt it was the only way.

After I held her, Mark had his turn. His big, strong hand covered her whole backside. Curled up, she fit in his palm, Even holding her, it was unimaginable that this little baby could grow into a healthy child. A few minutes after cradling her, the nurse came to return Ella to her Isolette. She couldn't maintain her body temperature, and she started to sound alarms; it was enough for today. I pumped in the pumping room, handed my milk over to the nurse, visited the cafeteria for lunch, and then sat with Ella the rest of the day. Day rolled to evening, but it was always tough to tell the time in that side of the NICU with no windows, lit up day and night—like being in Vegas without the fun. The cold reality of quitting time approached, and I broke down for the hundredth time in a few days. Mark held my hand, and we left. We worked out a plan to stay at my cousin's summer home a few miles down the road, which gave us a home base close to Ella for a few months.

Getting settled at my cousin's house, we made dinner, and I had a glass of wine for the first time since before pregnancy. I thought it would have miraculous powers and somehow clear my worry for an hour, but no luck. The bottom of the glass felt the same as the top. There was no moving out of my feelings, even if temporarily.

We finished dinner, I pumped and hoped for sleep, only a few hours later to be nudged by my alarm to get up and pump again, and then again at 6 a.m., and then I was up. I showered and headed to the NICU while Mark headed back to work at the office. Our new parental jobs had begun. Mark had to continue to make money, and I had to keep Ella alive.

Arriving at the NICU, Ella was doing fine, but her belly was really distended. They had begun feeding her one to two milliliters of breast-milk through the feeding tube. The breastmilk was mixed with formula to add calories to help her grow. Apparently, babies that tiny do not grow fast enough with just breast milk, so they create different recipes to help them put on weight more quickly. Her immature, small stomach had to be stretched with food and wasn't efficient at digesting. Formula is made from cow's milk, which preemies have a hard time digesting, and Ella had an especially hard time.

Her belly was bulged out like a balloon, and she was desatting quite a bit. Alarm after alarm sounded. I was too scared to hold her, so I sat with her through the alarms. The neonatologist came around with a team of residents, which happened every morning, and they created a plan for Ella daily. Today, he seemed concerned and ordered X-rays for her stomach, explaining the risk of NEC. If she had NEC, she would be rushed into surgery where they would remove the part of her intestine that was infected, but if not caught soon enough, it would cause death. The "soon enough" part meant within hours, like they have to catch that infection within hours of when it starts in order to save the baby.

I sat as they took pictures of her belly to make sure she didn't need surgery or worse. After about an hour, a resident came by and said it was just gas; she had digestion issues but no signs of infection. Temporary relief, a moment of reprieve. I left to go pump and eat lunch, which was my daily break, and then I returned to sit with her. By evening, Mark came in, and I left to go stretch my legs and rest at home, which really just meant a night of broken sleep and pumping.

One day in those first couple of weeks, bleary-eyed, I walked to the NICU, scrubbed in, went to see Ella, and her Isolette was gone. Mic drop. A nurse caught my eyes and said, "Oh honey, Ella is on the other side of the NICU now, a feeder and a grower." Shocked, I looked at her in disbelief. She wasn't two pounds yet, but she was now on the carpeted side of the NICU, the side with windows! I crossed over into the feeder/grower side, which felt like stepping into a spa compared to the other side, and found Ella. She was through the riskiest part of her stay, no apnea, still desatting but not that bad.

A new nurse approached me and said, "Hey, what's your story?" I guess many NICU babies are premature due to substance use, so when babies come through without disabilities that are that tiny, it is unusual. She and I chatted, and I told her my story. She then said, "Wait, you are Mark Boedges' wife? This is Mark's baby?" And I said yes. She explained that her mom had been following Mark and his work for a while, and she was an artist herself. We just clicked, and she became my primary in the NICU, my lifeline, really. Nurses are the circulatory system of the NICU, delivering nourishment in the form of care, medicine, intuition, encouragement, and skill. The doctors are more of the skeleton, and when they are working well together, they create an efficient vessel that holds these babies until they are hopefully healthy enough to go home. I had a buddy, a coach now—I didn't feel so lonely.

That day, a new neonatologist came around for rounds with his team. They reported that Ella's iron was low, and that she may need a blood transfusion, which sometimes happens. However, her levels were right at the point that they would order a transfusion. I offered my blood, but they couldn't take it, because it needed to be cleaned. She would have a donor. There was also concern about getting her to gain weight. The team of residents and PAs, along with a nutritionist, brainstormed a plan and decided to feed her a mixture of formula, protein, and olive oil in breastmilk to help Ella grow.

She was now a "feeder and grower," but she wasn't good at it yet. Every morning, we would all wait to see if she had grown an ounce, which was the desired gain. We would strip her down to nothing and put her on the scale, and, holding my breath, I would wait for the flashing number to stop still to see if she had reached her target. If she gained an ounce or more, I breathed a sigh of relief. If not, I would be sent into a spiral of despair that she was not getting enough nutrition. It all hung on one fucking number.

She now had also progressed to sleeping on her back, no more belly sleeping. Because back sleeping is supposedly the safest sleep position, they stop allowing belly sleeping after the first couple of weeks. Haha, a sleep position implies a baby sleeps. Not our Ella. Feeder and grower? Yes. Sleeper? No. Now being placed on her back, she began having awful reflux, which made her desat more than she had before. Many babies have reflux, but preemies have it because the muscle going into their stomach is not fully developed. On top of that, she had a stridor, which is when a floppy tissue above the vocal cords falls into the entry of the airway, causing a high-pitched sound on inhale. It is similar to the sound you might make if you tense your throat and inhale really quickly when surprised, but for preemies, it just happens every time they breathe in.

Reflux for Ella and some other preemies is not just like reflux regular babies have. It is like a volcano erupting. And when this happened after Ella ate, it would flood her entire sinus passages and choke her to the point that she would get dusky from her inability to breathe. I would have to mad dash it to get a sinus sucker and suction her out so that she could breathe again. After feeding her and I held her upright for a couple of hours to ensure that, when I put her on her back in the Isolette, she had the best chance of not spitting up. Generally, if she was lying on her back and spit up, she would choke. I held her upright as much as I could after feedings, and Mark would take the evening shift, but at some point, she had to be laid down at night. Mark and I became the masters of belly massage to aid digestion. I've never been so excited about poop in my entire life. Every diaper that I changed on Ella, I had to report to the nurse what was inside. This was a new part of my job description: mommy of a preemie, meaning poop reporter.

Ella was the only baby awake all night in the NICU. The nurses would tell me that they would hold her when they could. A crying baby that wants to be held but doesn't have other issues is generally a low priority. This broke my heart to know she would be awake at night crying with no one to hold her.

One morning, I came in, and Ella looked terrible. Her color was ashen, skin splotchy, and her monitors were dinging wildly. She was having trouble breathing and keeping her oxygen levels up. The visiting nurse rushed over, and she said, "We had an incident." I looked wide-eyed at her. What exactly was an "incident"? She continued. "I fed Ella this morning," which meant she got out the measured amount of milk. It goes into a tube that hangs from inside the Isolette, attached to the tube that goes through her mouth to her belly. The tube has fine lines on it, and the number by her lip is significant, because it is fitted perfectly to go down her esophagus into her belly. The nurse double-checks the number before every feeding to make sure the tube hasn't moved.

The nurse stammered, "I fed her, but she started alarming and desatting, and when I came to check on her, I saw that her tube was not in the right place." I glared. She forgot to check the tube. She fed Ella, and the misplaced tube, further up her esophagus, basically fed milk to her lungs. I started crying, shaking. For the first time, I realized, Ella was not just battling her own design, but she was up against everyone's humanness. All of these people were just human, and they made mistakes. I felt so powerless, I wasn't there to help her, and I had to continue trusting these people to keep her alive. I did not leave Ella's side at all that day, and held her the entire time, and prayed and prayed that she did not develop pneumonia from aspirating formula-laden breast milk, which is a common complication. Pneumonia in preemies can be life-threatening.

Later that day, I asked to speak with the head nurse. A first-time NICU mom, I wasn't sure how this whole thing worked, but this nurse made a mistake that could have been deadly, and this was a day after I had found a tiny cap that she had left in Ella's Isolette, a fucking choking hazard! I sat with the head nurse and told her about the two potentially life-threatening errors made by this nurse, and she let me know that all the nurses had adequate training to care for the babies. Furious, I left the meeting. I had heard of nurses getting fired, but it was like I couldn't even advocate for Ella's best care. From that day forward, I knew it was absolutely essential to get her out of the NICU as soon as possible.

A few days after that, the lactation consultant came by, and at about thirty weeks gestation, Ella started latching on to my breast to begin to learn how to nurse. The suck-swallow reflex is immature in preemies, but it is like Ella knew what she needed to do, and she began to work out how to suck and not drown on breast milk fairly quickly. When I started nursing her, they would weigh her before and after a feeding to see how much milk she got from nursing. Nursing versus bottle-feeding is tricky, because it is more complex and requires more energy, which impedes growth. To further complicate it, the doctors couldn't be sure how much Ella was getting while nursing like they could with a measured bottle. So, although they encourage nursing, they don't really promote nursing, because they can't control it. The benefits for preemies that can nurse are exponential; their development and neurobiology benefit. To assess the feeding, nursing was broken down to a mathematical equation to "prove" that Ella was getting enough milk. So goddamn stressful. Then, because I chose to nurse and not bottle-feed initially, Ella was still tube-fed in between nursings. You can't give a preemie the option of breastfeeding and bottle-feeding simultaneously while they are learning; they will choose the bottle, because it is more straightforward, and they have to master the more difficult task first. Then the challenge becomes determining how long to only nurse her before introducing a bottle. It took more time, Ella grew so slowly, and the doctors and insurance companies didn't like that. After a certain amount of time, the insurance companies want the babies out of NICU. Fatten them up with formula and get them out.

Teaching Ella to nurse in the NICU was not some picturesque bonding moment between us. I had let go of many fantasies up to this point; what was one more? Nursing, pumping, latching early on all took place with a small audience. Supposedly, nursing is this natural thing that we can do anytime, anywhere, but bless those moms. As a new mom, I would be sitting in a nursing chair with Ella, with some small curtain kind of pulled around our little section in the NICU, and a lactation consultant and/or nurse would be there helping position Ella on my breast. A nurse would ask, "Can I touch you?" and then wrangle my nipple into Ella's mouth, shoving it so far down her throat I thought she would choke. We did this every time until I could get the hang of it myself or try to help place and hold a nipple shield on my nipple while Ella learned to latch. Meanwhile, other nurses might pop in, along with doctors, other moms, dads, and caregivers visiting other Isolettes. My idea of quietly nursing and bonding was blown up. Forget quiet moments of intimacy and connection with my new baby; this was more like being stretched, pulled, and displayed like a Gumby toy, providing food for a sick baby. No pressure! (Did I mention that milk flow is significantly affected by stress, prematurity, and lack of sleep?) Every win felt like an enormous uphill battle; nothing came easy for us in those early days. I still don't know who the bigger fighter is, me or Ella?

#

There are a few tasks that NICU babies must accomplish before they are allowed to go home. Every NICU is a little different, but at our hospital, she had to maintain her body temperature outside the heated Isolette, eat on her own without a feeding tube for an entire twenty-four hour period via bottle, nursing, or both, no desats or apnea events for seven successive days, and she had to keep her vitals up while sitting in a car seat for a certain amount of time. These tasks may seem minor, but these things all mean life or death outside of the NICU to a micro-preemie. Some NICUs will send babies home with heart monitors and breathing monitors, but not our hospital. They said if she completed these tasks, she would not need extra monitoring at home.

Ella got stronger by the day and had few true apnea events after her first week of life. Her reflux was mainly what was causing her desatting toward the end of her NICU stay. I can remember Ella had passed the tests and was ready to begin her seven days' countdown to go home, so we got moved to the back room where I could sleep on some fold-out plastic bench next to her to allow her to nurse for twenty-four hours. Two days before she was set to go home, only two more days to go with good vitals, and we would be free from this place!

I fed her and really needed to go eat lunch. My nurse that day knew Ella was notorious for reflux, and if she laid down too long after eating would gag and desat. I took a chance and ran down to eat lunch, because I was incredibly hungry. When I returned, Ella was a mess, and the nurse looked entirely downtrodden. Ella had been crying, but it was busy, so the nurse had left her, and she had had a reflux incident that gagged her and caused a desat. Nooooooooooo! My heart sank to my feet. We were going to have to restart the seven-day countdown all over again. Noooooooo! I was sobbing. This would be Ella's first countdown restart. For other parents, their babies had countdowns restarted multiple times. Sometimes a baby would get to day six and have an event that would restart the counter, and it was traumatic for everyone. A seven-day countdown could take a month to complete successfully.

To this day, I'm not sure why, but the neonatologist who was on that day said that an event caused by eating would not restart her "count-down." What? You are an angel! I could have kissed her. After that, Ella did fine, and a couple of days later, we put her tiny body, all four pounds, into a car seat and took her in the car for two hours home. *We are free*, I thought; *we are free*. Little did I know . . .

16

Art Must Be Made, Sacrifices Ensue

Burlington, Vermont: July 2013

My extended family had rented a lake house for a big family vacation. My brothers had traveled in, and it was supposed to be a fun celebration. All along, I had this fantasy that we would get out of NICU on time to go on this family trip and kick back and relax. We accomplished goal number one, get Ella home by early July, but the relaxed vacation never happened. We got Ella home, but we could not put her down even for five minutes. She would cry and cry or have reflux, turn blue, need suctioning; I would freak out, and then we would settle down. This went on twenty-four hours a day.

That first week, we attempted to take her to the vacation lake house, and it was ninety degrees. We were all outside. I left her with Mark in her car seat while I went to play in the lake with my family. When I returned, maybe a half hour later, Ella was pale. I pulled her out to nurse her, but she was floppy. Floppy like when someone is dead asleep, you lift up their arm, and it falls back to the bed with no tone floppy. In the NICU, this was a test for significant distress. Shit! We just got out of NICU! Ella is floppy! My thoughts started spinning. *She must be dehydrated, or maybe overheated, or maybe sick with a virus, or perhaps I don't know what, but we are in the middle of nowhere, so I have to think of something.*

Returning to the hospital seemed imminent. I quickly got into the car with her, immediately flipped on the max A/C, and began trying to nurse her and bottle-feed her. Finally, she began to lose her flop and started to nurse. This was the kind of kid Ella was. She was perpetually pushed to her physical limits daily by sheer virtue of being a micropreemie, and somehow, she would recover from the crisis.

I have some dream that this physical confidence will be her North Star through life. Now, when she throws a tantrum that would probably make Napoleon look tame, I think to myself, *This is the spirit of a survivor.* And I cannot take that away from her; her spirit is why she is here today. Her grit and will are why she is here—that and modern medicine. Had I had my babies fifty years earlier, they would all most likely not have survived. I think about that privilege sometimes, just by the nature of the era I was born into.

When they discovered surfactants for preemies, babies like mine had a chance at life. Surfactant is the chemical that helps keep the lungs open, working, and buoyant. Unfortunately, tiny preemies don't make surfactant, so their lungs do not work well, and they often can't breathe. It was frequently the cause of death for early babies before the 1980s, when they started administering it to preemies. These thoughts of how fragile the shifting tides of life can be remind me to stay present. No moment with my daughter is guaranteed then or now, and I am not entitled to any of it; it happens as a blessing of grace. That is a reality I generally live with day in and day out.

After Ella's birth and two-month NICU stay, our failed attempt at a vacation, and almost returning to NICU days after getting released, Mark resumed his regular schedule at his IT job. As a result, the gallery and art business suffered. The juggling we had been doing was now just a one-handed toss. The gallery was barely open enough to justify the rent expense. We couldn't be open because we were not in town for the past two months and too busy with a one-pound, twelve-ounce preemie to worry about it. One day, sitting in the NICU, shortly before bringing Ella home, we were talking about what we were going to do.

There was enough cash in the business account to cover the rent for one more month (July) and a little extra. It seemed hopeless, and the subsequent decision seemed obvious: close the gallery and begin again when we had more time and money.

Instead, I told Mark, in times like this, when you feel like you need to hold your cash, you need to spend it on making more sales. So yup, fuck it, take all that money and buy an ad. He thought I was crazy, but I insisted we buy advertising now. We hadn't been around to produce energy around the gallery. We must declare ourselves like Ella did. So Mark took the cash and bought one ad.

One week after Ella came home, Mark had a trip scheduled for Door County Plein Air in Wisconsin. After all we had been through, of course, he planned to cancel. Ella had been home seven days, still weighed four pounds, and needed to be held 24/7. Figuring out a sleeping situation for a newborn is challenging enough, but Ella would not allow me to put her in the co-sleeper. The first few nights, I would nurse her, put her down, she would scream and have reflux, I would pick her back up, and repeat for hours. In the morning, I would sleep for a few hours while someone else held her, and then she would sleep. It was a disaster.

Too scared to co-sleep and not sure how we could support her and get sleep ourselves, we moved this giant, oversized chair and ottoman into our bedroom. We took shifts, three hours at a time. One parent would sleep in the bed, and the other would put Ella on their chest and surround her with a nest of pillows. This was not totally safe, but we really had no choice; she wouldn't sleep any other way. I was petrified of SIDS, but we needed sleep. If she continually cried, she burned too many calories, resulting in little to no weight gain. We did this routine for FOUR MONTHS! The rest was horrific, and sometimes I would get this incredible urge that I had to move. I couldn't sit in the chair any longer, and I would resist the urge to move as long as possible and then tap out. It was the best we could all do.

Perhaps it was the lack of sleep that left me with poor judgment, but when the Wisconsin trip came, I told him, "Go. The business has suffered, we have suffered; if you want this to work, you have to sacrifice and go and make money." Somewhat reluctantly, the next day, he took vacation time from work, drove to Wisconsin, and participated in the event. He painted under pressure for an entire week, attempting to get a masterpiece. By week's end, he was exhausted but rejuvenated. He hadn't been able to dive into painting like that in months, and it gave him clarity that he would really love to be able to paint full-time. It was a nice reminder, but the real challenge was to have his enthusiasm translate to a paycheck to keep the gallery afloat.

Back home, we all waited. The night of the show had arrived, and we sat eager for news. Did he pull it off? Was this trip a bust? Is the art career over? In the evening, I got a text from him: "Babe, my work sold out before the show opened in less than five minutes." So much of our journey to this point had felt like a slog through quicksand, and every time we reached the other side, it just felt like thank goddess we hadn't drowned. This was the first moment that felt like an actual win. The sales were enough to help him continue working as an artist for a few more months. Later that evening, he was awarded Best in Show, Artists' Choice Award, and sold out the rest of his work. That was the sign we needed, but it took some grueling decisions about our commitment to our life choices. This felt like that decision point where, had he decided not to go to the show, he would have given up after years working as an artist, right before his big break. The awards not only gave him confidence but lots of good press, which is critical to an artist's success. Big magazines were talking about him, which is basically free advertising.

Later that summer, he also won Best in Show at the Scottsdale Salon of Fine Art. His summer success padded the bank account enough to give us the hope to plan for the next step, which was Mark quitting a full-time, salaried, benefited, pensioned job to be a full-time artist. Now, if you read this and think, *That is crazy!* It is, it still is. Who gives up all that security willingly? Who the hell is willing to let go of a pension nowadays? Especially when there is absolutely no family financial backing, like zero . . . no trust fund, no inheritance, no extravagant down payments for houses, no cars, etc. It is all possible, but I always had this deep understanding that we had to want it so bad that we were willing to literally jump off a cliff and hope that the chutes opened. It is a daily friggin' bungee jump.

At the crux of it, for me, managing fear around uncertainty is the root of entrepreneurship. But although the uncertainty feels like it is about money, I think it is about life in general. There are no guarantees in life, but we develop a sense of safety when we create a schedule and maintain some regularity through work, school, and routine. It allows us to feel in control, and that helps us feel safe. Being self-employed is like the opposite of that, at least for now. We are constantly deciding what shows to do, what ads to run, what workshops to teach, where to teach, etc. It can feel unsafe, and usually, what helps me is remembering that I have already lived my worst fear: losing a child. When I sit with that reality, I can face most daily fears living with uncertainty.

Getting through winter with Ella was stressful. At about six months old, I moved her into bed with me and nursed her at night while we slept side by side. The big concern was that she stay virus free all winter; not a single cold could come through our house, because she could end up back in the NICU if she got sick. As a result, we never took her anywhere in public for that entire winter season. If we went out, we would undress at the door when we came in and "scrub in" to wash away as many germs as possible. It was isolating and lonely to have a tiny newborn at home and no way to connect with the community. Even the holidays were limited to avoid exposure and keep her safe.

During the winter, I was also able to start feeding her some solid food, which was a relief. I was no longer her primary food source, and it felt like an enormous burden had been lifted. However, she only gained a pound a month in the first few months home, and that is considered failure to thrive in the baby world, although nobody said it outloud. She was way too small. It makes me cringe to this day to think about my arguments with the neonatologist over breastfeeding Ella. When I brought her in for visits, and she was gaining a quarter of a pound a week, he told me that I was not producing enough milk or that my milk was not "rich" enough in nutrients to help her grow. They had done the math on how many calories she needed. I was feeding her one to two bottles of breast milk with added formula plus breastfeeding, which, on paper, should have been more than enough nutrition. Instead, she defied the number and science in almost every way, I suppose.

I dove into the research about stuffing preemie babies with formula to make them grow faster. Although it makes everyone happy to get them on a growth chart, the research shows that many micropreemies are predestined for excessive weight gain later in life, and breastfeeding can help negate that. At one point, the doctor told me that I would cause permanent brain damage and inhibit her intellectual development if I kept nursing instead of switching to an all-formula diet. For her, an all-formula diet would have provided a significant excess in calories and would affect her digestion dramatically. From day one, she could not digest formula; that never got easier for her.

So, against the pleading of the neonatologist, I followed my gut, and I stuck with the plan of one breast milk / formula bottle a day and kept nursing her. At six months, I started giving her solids, mainly apples cooked and pureed with olive oil and rice cereal. Even with solids, she continued to gain a pound a month for her first year of life. She weighed in at a whopping twelve pounds at twelve months. She was small as hell but developmentally appropriate and walking like a champ! In my gut, I knew that formula-feeding Ella, when it caused her so much digestive distress in the NICU to the point that they thought she had NEC, was not the answer. I had to resist giving in to the pressure of a known expert to attempt to give my baby what I thought was best for her. She did not make it onto any growth chart until the age of two, and now at the age of eight, she is tiny, on the chart somewhere. At this point, I could care less; she is happy, healthy, creative, and brilliant.

In the face of knowledge from experts, like doctors in the medical system, I found it the hardest to stay true to my instinct, but I did. Of course, only time will tell, but I don't think the medical system has all the answers, and I don't think "fatten them up" is the answer for all preemies to thrive.

The sad part is trauma brings us out of our bodies and up into our heads, away from sensation in the body. With trauma, bodily sensation becomes too overwhelming. Still, the only way to follow a "gut" instinct is to tap into feelings found in our bodies. Without all of my training, I would not have had the insight to stay true to my "gut" and take time amidst the hospital chaos, weather through the loss of Sophie Joy, my pregnancy with Ella, or our NICU stay, to be still and listen. Stillness is required to decode the sensations of the body, which give us our truth. The body never lies, but our minds will tell stories.

\#

For the entirety of our marriage, Mark has worked full-time IT and painted after work and on weekends, pursuing the dream. We are both reasonably independent people, so we could negotiate all of this before children and still find our way. Now, we had a preemie baby. I was working part-time, and Mark was working full-time while painting, basically also full-time. I was exhausted. I felt like, after everything, something had to give, and we had to give it a try. I could not live my life this way, working toward a dream that we would never have the courage to pursue. So, it may have been really one of the only ultimatums I have ever given Mark, but I said he had to choose, now or never. We decided to have a family, and now there was no time to balance all interests, work, etc.

In the face of realizing we were at capacity, something had to shift. We didn't retreat; we decided to go for it. Well, maybe I decided to go for it! Ha! I began telling everyone I knew that Mark was quitting his job in May to pursue art. Before he had really decided he was ready, we picked a date, and then we just started talking about it. That is usually how things happen in our house—select a date with the end goal in mind, then start talking about it. The plans unfold, and sometimes the goal changes, but it starts the process. To achieve great things, I must begin to tell the story about it before it ever happens, much like Ella and the doctors at twenty-four weeks. Some call it manifesting: Start with the sensation that you want to end up with, the feeling, then start embodying that first. Start talking about the outcome first. This process requires faith—faith that things will begin to unfold and happen as I set my course through intention. So, perhaps begrudgingly, Mark began to tell the story, too, that he would become a full-time artist in May.

We kept talking about it, generating excitement. The moment we had been working toward since shortly after we met was now almost upon us. Two weeks out from Ella's birthday in early May, he gave his notice. We planned to cash out his pension to float us for a few months, and the rest was up to us. Our "MayDay" came and went, and that was it—bye-bye IT. They had cake as a going-away at the office, Ella was one and healthy, and shit! We were off!

17

Expect The Unexpected

Burlington, Vermont: July 2014

Between summer and fall 2014, right after quitting IT, Mark won Best in Show at Wayne Plein Air, Artist's Choice at Door County Plein Air, and Best in Show with the American Impressionist Society, along with a feature article in *Art of the West*. He continued to get accolades and recognition for his paintings. A combination of years of hard work, luck, and privilege was paying off.

Mark was traveling quite a bit between plein air events and getting material for gallery pieces. We were busy shuffling Ella care between the two of us and our work, but it all seemed doable. I would cram in a full-time therapist schedule into two or two and a half days while he watched Ella, and the other days he worked while I took care of her.

In July, a little over a year of keeping Ella safe, healthy, and alive, seven years after our baby journey began, the unexpected happened. My period was light in June, and I didn't think much of it at first, because I had not had a regular cycle since Ella was born. But I started to feel tired and nauseous by July. I thought, *Ugh, this is weird; this kind of feels like pregnancy, but really there is no way. So many years of perfect timing and trying to conceive, there is no way I just randomly got pregnant.* Mark was headed out for a week of travel in mid-July and would be gone for ten days. My mind started to unravel: *What if? Fuck, fuck, fuck, what if? No, there is no way! But? Gah! What do I do? Do I get a pregnancy test? Do I tell Mark? Should I just wait and see? I mean, wait and see in the past has generally meant no viable pregnancy.*

I landed on buying a pregnancy test just in case, and then would decide what to do one step at a time. I brought the test home and half-heartedly took it and left it on the sink, not thinking much of it. Then, a half hour later or so, I glanced at the test: two little lines. SHIT!!

Ella was still not sleeping through the night. Hell, she was still nursing numerous times a day. She weighed around thirteen pounds and was walking, but we were all maxed out! People would see her out and just reach down and pick her up, because she was the tiniest little walking being most people had ever seen. I would literally have to take Ella back from strangers' hands. It was like the combination of her pixie-blue eyes and petite stature drew people to her; her eyes still have that effect. She would stare, like uncomfortably stare, and most people would say, "I feel like she is staring into my soul." My favorite response was "She is." Because, really, she is an old soul, she wanted to be here, and I think she has work to do. What that is? I can only imagine, but I have been blessed as guardian of this angel. Now, can I stand the possibility of guarding another soul, no matter how short their little karma is? I don't know.

I told Mark we were pregnant again, and eyes wide, his jaw dropped. He said, "No way."

I said, "Yeah, yeah, way, but we know how this usually goes."

Ah, there was Hope again on her chariot, but what if? *What if, for some reason, this pregnancy holds on? Like Ella? And then we are facing NICU again five months from now? Newly self-employed with a seventeen-month-old preemie and a sick newborn in NICU. What if I am on bed rest again with Ella at just a year?* The fear, panic, and relentless what-ifs sent me into a typhoon of worry that not even Goddess Sophia could slow. Mark was planning on leaving for ten days, which, if this dragged out, would be ten days more into a pregnancy. *Also, what if I miscarry while Mark is away and I'm alone with Ella? I'll have to tell someone, but who? Can I face another miscarriage?*

I scheduled an appointment for the following week. The doctor did an ultrasound, and I was pregnant; there was a heartbeat. That little bean was somewhere between six and eight weeks. *WHAT?! How is this even possible?* I spent years trying to get pregnant on purpose. I cried; I felt stuck. I wanted something so badly for years, and now I wasn't sure this was what I wanted. I was so broken from all the pain of pregnancy, childbearing, and NICU, I wasn't sure I had the stamina for this work at this moment. I felt so defeated, confused, ashamed that I was in this position and had no idea what to do.

During the consult, we were weighing our options, and the doctor said, "I just spent a year in the NICU with a baby, and that baby never made it home." I sat there staring at her, thinking. I had run through what I thought were the most hellacious outcomes, but that one seemed to have evaded me until now. A year in the NICU and your baby still dies—holy crap. I had imagined a baby dying at birth, before birth, shortly after birth, like the little baby whose parents only came to see it for a few minutes every day. She was next to Ella but off in a cubby away from the rest because she was extremely sick. Her monitors were always going off, and one day she was rushed off to surgery. The last time I saw her parents, only about a week after Ella's birth, the doctors were consulting with them alone in the waiting area, closed lobby, outside of the NICU. I'm sure they were telling them the outcomes looked terrible. After that, I never saw any of them again.

That baby lived a few days in the NICU. I had not thought of a baby surviving, fighting for a year, sick and in pain, and then dying. I think that might have just sealed my decision. As painful as the guilt was of potentially terminating a pregnancy that had a slim chance of viability, I could not live through the pain of bringing a sick baby into this world to suffer along with Ella. Yet again, a parenting decision no mom or dad should have to make. I have infinite compassion for moms and dads that get news that a pregnancy will not thrive, but the baby is still alive inside mom. It is an impossible decision that is so personal and painful.

The OB said that her job was to bring babies into the world, and a different department would help with termination if that was what we wanted. Termination was not what we wanted, but we were still so shell-shocked from our losses, birth of Ella, Ella surviving a year of life, that the idea and possibility of opening ourselves up to more pain was intolerable. See, this was the shift: No longer did I have the fantasy of a healthy living baby at the end of a pregnancy. All I could think about was the pain and loss amid trying to help Ella stay healthy. It was no longer just Mark and me; we had Ella now, too. And how would all of this impact her? We left as confused as we went in, with no clear answers or decisions.

Literally, the next day, I started bleeding. First, it started light, but then I began to pass tissue, like clumps of liver. I feel like I must share that detail, because the judgment around termination decisions is so harsh. Clearly, my body was rejecting this pregnancy.

I called the doctor. "I am miscarrying."

She said, "You never know."

I said, "I know, I know my body, and I know that this is not going to stick." So now, I was facing a miscarriage at home with Ella while Mark was traveling for work. Hadn't I already been through hell? And for anyone thinking, *What were you doing for birth control?* You would be right: Not much, which in hindsight, as this story progresses, may have been foolish, but at thirty-seven with all the fertility issues, I just did not see the point.

The day before Mark was to leave for his painting event, we went back to the "other" department to do a D&C so I wouldn't face a miscarriage alone with a one-year-old while he was gone. Things continued to get tricky and more painful. We arrived for the visit, and the doctor let me know that if there was no heartbeat, then the procedure would be coded as a D&C and covered by insurance. If they did an ultrasound and there was a heartbeat, even if I was miscarrying, insurance wouldn't pay for it.

I asked, "Can we just skip the ultrasound?"

She said, "No."

Not doing an ultrasound is not an option, because "they" have to know how to code it for insurance purposes. So, we went in and had the ultrasound, I was still bleeding heavily, but goddammit, there was still a heartbeat. *FUCK THIS, fuck this universe, fuck all of this.* I had made it, at that point, my entire thirty-seven years without a termination for a pregnancy. I had never faced this dilemma, as many women do. Now, after being through hell and back, I was faced with the impossible decision: Do I continue and naturally miscarry? Or not? And potentially end up with another stillborn child? Early delivery, like twenty-four weeks? Or a year in the hospital and still a dead child?

In my being, even though there was a heartbeat, I felt that with the cramping, bleedings, and passing tissue that this pregnancy was not viable. If Mark was not leaving the next day, I would have waited to miscarry at home. Realistically, Mark had to go, because he had to make money; staying and waiting this out wasn't an option. We proceeded. I took some valium, and they took me to a back room. No joke, this procedure is done in a modified back closet at the hospital. There really were boxes and things around the room, and the entrance was separate from the regular maternity visits. The room was darkish. I laid down on the table like I had so many times before. Two women were assisting me, and the procedure lasted maybe two minutes before the doctor declared, "You are no longer pregnant."

I can still smell and taste that moment of grief and guilt. I gathered myself with a cleansing breath, and I walked out to the waiting area to Mark and Ella. I felt guilty as hell for a long time. Who was I to decide how that pregnancy was to go? If I let nature take its course, I would have likely finished miscarrying alone with Ella at home. How come I couldn't do that? The honest answer was I did not have it in me. Keeping Ella alive over the last year was all I could handle. Keeping one baby alive. We got home a few hours later, I rested, and Mark prepared for his trip.

I even wondered if, when I told my story, could I tell this part of it? Like, who in my life might judge me for this choice? Judge me harshly? But this is the whole story, no filters, and I felt like so much of my suffering came from not appreciating the entire tale of motherhood, because it is usually not all told. So, since I'm telling my story, I feel like the service is in the grueling unedited details of journeying to momma-hood, especially the shame-ridden ones. We all have our stories, and if we all felt we could tell them completely, I think we would not all grieve alone, but together, knowing we are all living through it.

There is so much controversy over pregnancy termination. When I think about termination, even for myself, I think of my teenage friends who got pregnant and felt they were too young to have children. I often don't think of the mom who just got diagnosed with cancer and needs treatment or will die, or the mom who just found out their baby won't survive outside of the womb; the rape victim, or me, who had been through so many bad, natural miscarriages, stillbirth, and a one-pound, twelve-ounce preemie, facing a potential miscarriage, stillbirth, or worse with a one-year-old and fully self-employed family. We are the women who are making termination choices, too, not just the impulsive teenager. We are all far more complex than the stereotypes, and having been where I was and am now, I would never interfere with a woman's right to choose.

I saw so many drug-addicted babies in the NICU, babies that I now know will grow up likely addicted and spend most of their lives addicted. Opiate-addicted babies cry incessantly; they cannot be soothed. Doctors administer small doses of opiates initially to comfort them, and I overheard a doctor say that the natural remedy is holding, physically holding these babies, but guess who was there to hold them? No one. These babies cried, and no one was there to hug them. These moms and dads, for whatever reason, perhaps still addicted themselves, weren't there. I think this goes on for generations. That is another stereotype in the NICU: Many babies there are preemies because of substance abuse. Premature birth is highly correlated with maternal substance abuse.

Some volunteers come in to hold babies in the NICU, which maybe I will do after my own babies get older, but it is not enough. NICU babies like Ella need twenty-four-hour kangaroo care. I think Ella would have done better if I could have stayed with her overnight. I believe, to this day, she might not have slept through the night because I would have to leave her there. It was unnatural, leaving a two-pound baby in a plastic box, hooked up to monitors overnight with strangers. Yes nurses, but they were strangers. And although Ella would cry, she wasn't in an acute situation, so sometimes, if nothing more serious was going on, they would pick her up, but sometimes not.

I had to get my sleep, if you could call it that; I had to set my alarm to pump every three hours overnight, and I have only slept a handful of nights all the way through since Ella was twenty-four weeks gestation. I totally understand why no sleep for a few days in a row gives one the opportunity for the "insanity plea" in a murder case. Sleeplessness is physically and emotionally grueling.

18

The Big Flop

Burlington, Vermont: January 2015

Well, after our termination in July, we were done having kids. We were pretty confident Ella was it, but we just did not have the energy to really think about it as a forever kind of decision. Even when Ella was delivered, they asked if I wanted my tubes tied, and I just couldn't bring myself to do it for whatever reason. I guess I wasn't ready. Mark would make comments about getting a vasectomy, and more so after July. It is funny to have gone through hell but still feel undecided about shutting down the baby factory for good. I have joked over the years that there is something about having kids that is just not rational. Now, my cycle is regular. Even on a good cycle, targeting pregnancy as a goal was like shooting skeet blindfolded, so fear alone was enough to prevent any reoccurrence in our sleep-deprived brains.

Ella was still not sleeping through the night and was nursing, so our bedroom was full. Sometime in December, we had a few minutes to ourselves for the first time in months—no joke here, months. We had a trip to Arizona toward the end of January for Mark's first two-person show at Legacy Gallery in Scottsdale. He had prepared all year for this show. We had ordered custom gold-gilded frames, put our heart, soul, and bank account on the line for this show! We would meet up with my brother and sister-in-law, who had just gotten out of the military and were RVing cross-country.

Right around the third week of January, I was feeling so tired, I asked Mark to get an air tester to check the air quality in our house. People, this is for real. I still laugh to myself about this discussion. I tested the air for radon and carbon monoxide. Sleep deprivation, nursing, and NICU trauma had elevated denial as a serious coping strategy in my emotional toolbox. After those tests came back negative, I had the thought. *Hmm-mmm.* Then one day in December: *I wonder if? No way, just no way.* We were headed on our trip cross-country. Even if I was pregnant, there was nothing to do about it anyway, and most likely, it wouldn't amount to much.

I cannot tell you how much money I have spent on pregnancy tests in this lifetime, and I am here to say, in my case, what a waste. Most of the time, if I had just waited, I might not even have known for sure that I was pregnant, and that would have been easier. So, I bought my hundredth pregnancy test and took it. *FUCK! Maaarrrrrrkkkk, you gotta see this!*

We both just stared at each other, no joy, dumbfounded; we were paralyzed. Then, the critical self-talk started. *How did we get here again? How did I let this happen? I can't go through a termination again, but I can't go through NICU again. How did we get to this place again?* I specialize in working with trauma, and it is not uncommon to uncon-sciously reenact traumatic situations in hopes of having a different out-come than we did in the original trauma. Like getting into the same type of relationship when you know the outcome—we so hope for a differ-ent one, but usually, it is the same replayed story. I know all this, and yet, still here I was, here we were, two foolish teenagers in a jam!

A couple of days later, we boarded a plane to Arizona with Ella in tow to attend Mark's first two-person show. This show was the buildup of Mark's career at this point. He had won many awards, and getting a two-person and/or one-person show was quite an achievement in the art world. We were so excited to meet collectors and the gallery owners. We arrived at our rental home and had a day to relax with my brother and sister-in-law. They planned to watch Ella while we attended the show. The evening of the show, we dressed in our finest outfits at the time, full of anticipation and joy, and headed out. We arrived early and met the gallery curator and then the owner. There were rooms in that gallery that contained artwork far more valuable than our first two homes combined. This was it—we had made it, I knew it! His career was made.

The show began, and many students came through to look at all of the art. Some collectors moseyed in and out of the rooms, and the evening wore on. One hour, then the next, then the next, and not one painting sold. The show adjourned, and heavy with despair, we left the event. Not one sale through opening night, not one, and meager attendance. The descriptors, defeat and despair, hardly touch the mood. The culmination of our work was lit in a dumpster fire, and not even the firefighters came to put it out. Mark does not handle defeat well, and I thought, *Eeeek—this might be the end.* We have had so many rough patches personally and professionally; we might have just met our match.

We met with the gallery director to discuss the evening the following day, and I was so upset. We talked about the marketing and the paintings, the content—should they be more Western in nature? Mark is an East Coast painter; what could we have done differently? He and I tossed ideas back and forth, and the bottom line wasn't more to know. The timing, the pieces, the prices, the content did not work. Before this show, we had decided to bump prices substantially, and I think that might have had something to do with the show's success. Still, it was necessary to cover framing and shipping costs. From that meeting, we agreed that one of the strongest pieces would go into the Scottsdale Art Auction for sale. The auction is prestigious, and there is a risk of having a piece in auction that doesn't sell, but it seemed like our only option. Apparently, auction prices used to influence the art market more than they do nowadays.

There is this dream fantasy that you can send a piece to auction, and it sells for one hundred times the current list price, but this happens basically never. It sometimes happens and launches an artist's career, but often the opposite happens; a piece sells for less than market value. So, with some hope and a little luck, we sent this bright, sunny, fall Vermont scene off to auction and waited. It was vibrant, the fall reds and yellows bounced off the canvas, and it could draw attention from across the room; the light was fun and playful.

The auction came and went, and no word. Then, shortly after the auction, Mark was teaching at the Scottsdale Art School, and someone congratulated him on his painting sale. Mark didn't know what he was talking about, and the artist told him his painting sold at auction. *YES!* We needed another nod from the universe. Mark did a little digging and found that it sold for double retail price! And here we are again experiencing the depths of despair to a moment of elation. This is the art world early in a career: extreme highs and lows.

Over the course of two years or so after that, almost all of Mark's pieces from the show sold. I guess the moral of the story is that there are continuous disappointments in art, which is a mild or major form of grief. Sadness that things did not turn out as we had hoped, fear for the future, and the unknown that comes with not getting a regular paycheck. Although challenging, Sophie Joy had prepared us for these moments. Living through unfathomable grief gave me the strength and power to forge ahead with Mark in our careers after significant setbacks and disappointments.

Meanwhile: flopping art show, Mark teaching, back to me incubating a potential new baby. Because it was so early in possible pregnancy, I didn't want to tell anyone, but of course, the universe had another plan. We were out hiking in the desert with my brother and sister-in-law, and the whole hike, I just kept thinking, *I'm going to vomit*. I had to keep slowing down, and finally, en route, I stopped and said, "I know this is awkward timing, and it probably doesn't mean much, but we had a positive pregnancy test right before we left Vermont." They all looked at me, and I don't even remember what they said, but it was sweet, because I didn't have to hide it anymore; I was openly tired and nauseous for the rest of the vacation.

19

Grace Anne

At this part of the story, we were all just wondering, *What on earth happened?* I think this is a question that happens a lot in stories about people having babies. My doctors, who had delivered so many high-risk babies, said they could watch and monitor, but they often just don't know that much about the outcome. The nurses would often ask the doctors about care recommendations, and a popular response from them would be "Yes, let's do it to ward off the evil spirits." Half jest, half we-don't-really-know. Comforting, right?

After our vacation, we returned to Dartmouth for an ultrasound, which confirmed we were eight weeks pregnant. We decided to just ride it out and scheduled our twelve-week visit. Life ticked on as usual, and the twelve-week ultrasound showed a baby growing and sized appropriately, so we just kept going. Neither one of us really believed there would be a baby at the end, but we didn't feel there were too many other options. We tested for PAPP-A to check the placenta and did all of the genetic testing, and the results all came back normal. At twenty or so weeks, we knew we were not in the same position we were with Ella and the other babies; this baby was doing her own thing. Luckily, most of the pregnancy was reasonably unremarkable; she continued to grow (so did I, I got huge!) and seemed healthy.

In early August, Mark was teaching day one of a three-day workshop in Waitsfield, VT. I was headed to Dartmouth for my regular daily stress test and thirty-six-week ultrasound. Her previous ultrasound was at thirty-two weeks, and she was in the fiftieth percentile size-wise, give or take. It was a Monday, August 10th, and her scheduled delivery was August 17th. She would be thirty-seven weeks at that point and safe to deliver. I had a slight inkling in the back of my mind: *What if today is the day?* So, listening to my "inklings," I had arranged for Ella to be taken care of by my brother and dad, so she did not have to make the trip to the hospital an hour and a half away. I asked my best friend Sarah to drive down with me "just in case" and so I didn't have to make the trip alone, She gladly came with me.

I went into the ultrasound, and I knew something was a little odd, because her head was so low that the ultrasound tech was having a hard time getting a good measurement, but it was reassuring to see her moving on the screen. After the tech took the pictures that she needed to, Sarah and I returned upstairs, waiting for my maternal-fetal medicine (MFM) appointment—the high-risk baby doctors.

One of my favorite MFM doctors was covering that day. She was the first doctor I met at the hospital a few years prior when we learned of our pregnancy with Ella. Eagerly waiting in the exam room, she entered, looked down at her clipboard, and said, "Well, your baby is looking tiny." Heart drop. I started crying immediately. Everything had been fine; how could this be?

The doctor reassured me that we were well along in the pregnancy, and we were in a totally different place than we were with Ella at twenty-four weeks. Then, she said, "Let me check your cervix to see if you are dilated and have started labor. If so, we deliver now." Oh goddess, please, please, please, I cannot do the wait-and-see, daily ultrasound, monitors, bed rest shit again.

She did the exam and smiled. "You are almost four centimeters dilated and fully effaced." WHAT?!?! I was dancing Nia the day before with my first Nia instructor, Jill, visiting from Colorado. Apparently, I was in labor with no noticeable contractions. So, I screamed for Joy; I was done with pregnancy three! She said, "Get over to Labor and Delivery now; your baby is coming tonight." I gave her a hug and rushed out to tell my bestie we were having a baby today!

In every phase of my life, I have had a best friend named Sara(h). Like #everydamnphase to the point that is a little eerie. My first best friend in life is named Sara. We met in kindergarten, and she lived right down the street from me. She was always a head taller than me; she topped out at six feet, and I at five feet, four inches. And she had a fondness for horses that has directed her whole life. I share that, because my bestie Sarah who came to the hospital with me that day is almost six feet and has a passion for horses. Although we met in Vermont, we grew up across the river from each other in Connecticut, and our moms had worked together over the years, but we found that out after we became friends.

Anyway, I ran out to tell Sarah that we had to call Mark and head to Labor and Delivery, and if Mark didn't get there in time, she was my person. I am so glad that she was there; she is also a therapist and has a knack for managing difficult situations with poise and grace.

We landed in labor and delivery, and they strapped a monitor on me to check for contractions. They needed to deliver before I went into hard labor, because after an old school C-section, there is a risk of uterine rupture during a vaginal delivery. I was having contractions, but I wasn't feeling them. My anxiety was through the roof. I thought my heart was going to pop out of my chest. I really could not imagine going through another C-section. You are awake on the table, strapped down, feeling the tug and pull on your abdomen.

As a trauma therapist, I know just about every trick in the book for naturally calming the nervous system, but I had little hope that any of those tricks would have worked right then. Maybe if I was a Buddhist monk, I could have accessed parasympathetic arousal through my breath, but, well, I guess I am not that well-practiced.

Mark was on his way. He called the day short and planned to arrive at the hospital an hour or so later. *Would she wait?* I was totally resigned to the fact that she, this mighty third daughter, was in charge of her own destiny, and she would decide who was at her birth, not I.

The anesthesiologist came in with a student and gave me the rundown. I told her I had horrible anxiety. Could she provide me with anxiety medication for delivery? Here is the kicker: If I took antianxiety meds, it could also affect the baby, making her lethargic, which means she could end up in the NICU. No, thanks—anxiety it is.

Contractions began to intensify and get closer together, Mark showed up, and it was go time. The anesthesiologist asked if I wanted to walk to the OR, and I told her I couldn't. My anxiety was so bad, my whole body was shaking; I was sweating, cold, nauseous, and dizzy. She began coaching me through breathing techniques. (I'm belly-laughing while writing; this still cracks me up.) I have my bestie in the room who is a therapist, I'm a trauma therapist, and the anesthesiologist read some exercise in a book and gave it to me. I played along, eye-rolling in my head to myself and my unwavering anxiety. She then started checking all my vitals, wondering aloud if my symptoms are from something more "organic." Again, eye roll, but she is thorough, I give her that.

They wheeled me into the OR, solo. I had to get the epidural and spinal on my own, and then they brought Mark in. I was hunched over on the table, totally naked in a whitewashed OR with who knows how many people prepping for surgery. They inserted the first big needle to numb me, then in went the epidural. There is always a slight risk of total paralysis because they misplace the epidural; this stuff is an art as well as a science.

Anyway, she threads the epidural, and I can feel it to the left of my spine, and I tell her it's in the wrong spot. She starts moving it around, and I keep saying, "No, that's not right, no." After wiggling and jiggling, the resident tells her to pull it out and start over. *ARE YOU FUCK-ING KIDDING ME?* I'm not terrible on needles, but this procedure is hellacious. I pulled out my breathing techniques like an enthusiastic yogi landed in India at an ashram for a life-changing metamorphosis. It helped a little through the sobs. I couldn't believe how hard this work was, bringing this baby into the world. My work as a momma is gritty; I have not had any free passes.

The anesthesiologist got it this time. They laid me down, curtain up. Mark was next to me. *Phew . . . he is here.*

They tested something cold on my stomach. I couldn't feel it, which meant I was numb, so they began to cut. About one minute into surgery, I felt like I was going to throw up. I couldn't move; I was strapped down. I interrupted the anesthesiologist talking about bologna sandwiches to tell her that I was about to vomit. She fumbled some weird tray to the side of my mouth and told me to turn my head. I was thinking, *What happens if I vomit lying strapped down on my back?* Luckily, I never found out. They hit me with some antinausea meds through the IV, and I was okay. Plus, now the morphine was starting to kick in, so I was loving everyone in the room. You see that in the movies, where people get dopey on meds and start telling everyone that they love them, but it is what happens. So maybe love and morphine have some common receptor sites in our nervous systems.

It felt like forever to get in through the scar tissue from my last C-section. They finally got to her, and we had a couple of names in mind, but I wasn't sure which to pick. They pulled her out and brought her to my head. Mark held her next to me and asked about her name. I said, "Grace?" And she smiled a big smile. That was it—she picked her name. The nurse took that little baby, just over five pounds, and latched her on my breast, and she nursed while the doctors tied my tubes (no more babies) and put me back together. Grace was here, just fine and seeming ginormous. *Relief, ahhh sweet relief.* The waiting was over. No NICU! Grace was a beautiful, almost-full-term, healthy baby girl. Ella's sister, that little love nugget, knew she needed to be here with her.

The funny thing about doing the impossible: I have gone through loss so much during pregnancy that I couldn't fathom that a positive outcome was possible. I now know it doesn't matter what my brain thinks is possible. My bestie always tells me that a Buddhist once said, "No thoughts are intelligent." Sometimes it is just about going through the steps one inch at a time, and my belief about my ability to do something and actually doing it are NOT the same thing. My brain does not have to understand how I will accomplish X. It, in fact, is often the last part of my physical existence to get on board when something scary or challenging is ahead. My heart and my body most often lead me through those challenges, not my head. And I just keep stringing together a few seconds of courage each time I do something hard; a few seconds is usually what it takes.

Grace's vitals were good; she was latching on well. We were all hanging out in the room after she was born. I was loopy from medication, and Grace cried every time the nurse tried to put her down in the clear plastic box next to me. After 10 or 11 p.m., Mark was tossing in the fold-out chair that they bring in for family members, not sleeping. I told him to get a hotel room for the night and get some sleep, because he had to get up early and teach his workshop. There is that tricky self-employment thing again. He had a workshop full of people visiting from all over to learn from him, so canceling the remainder of the workshop did not feel like an option. Baby born, and off you go!

All night, I tried—and the nurses tried—to put Grace down. The night nurse felt so bad that she rocked Grace for twenty minutes in the room, but she just cried. Finally, we all gave up, the nurse bolstered Grace up with some pillows on my chest, and she went to sleep. Both of my earthly babies are still this way. They like to be close to me to sleep, and it has taken years to get them to sleep in their own beds, which still only happens about 50 percent of the time. This is one of those things that I just figure will flush out over time. Sleeping and nursing had to occur on demand because my kids were so tiny; I never had the luxury of saying, "Oh, she is not hungry, she just wants to nurse for comfort" overnight. My babies always got to nurse when they wanted, because they had to grow.

Mark went off to teach the next day, and I was sent home early, family complete. When I see Grace and Ella together, I know that there is some connection that goes beyond what I might understand with my five senses. I believe that once Ella made it, Grace was always on the way.

20 |

The Owl Returns

Shelburne, Vermont: 2016

I had been teaching Nia for almost six months—Ella, age three, and Grace, age one—in a new space that is the old town hall in our small corner of Vermont. When you enter, it resembles a church; the foyer and the big wooden doors open to an expansive empty room with warm wood floors, churchlike windows lining the walls, and a stage at the far end. The ceilings are vaulted, and a balcony sits above the hall opposite the stage.

One morning, when I was teaching my Nia class, I noticed a mylar owl balloon in the upper right corner hanging out, watching over our class. There was another balloon floating, and it looked as if there maybe had been an event for young people, and two balloons got away to the upper ceiling. That day I just noticed, as I take notice of any owls that cross my path, and had a sweet thought that SJ was watching over us.

Two days later, during my next class, she was still hanging in the corner. After class, a student who did not know my story mentioned the balloon. I said, "Funny you mention her, because I have been noticing her as well," and told her my story. A few other students had gathered around to listen. I could feel the hum of our hearts, bodies, and souls joining in the truth of womanhood, relationships, caretaking, birthing, and creating, which all create an opening for beautiful things but also the gateway to profound grief. We are all grievers.

The following week, I entered town hall to teach class, and the owl balloon had lost her lift just enough to be hovering over the stage at eye level. Thinking my girls would enjoy her, I attached her to my purse by tying her pink ribbon around an arm strap on my bag. She stayed there the entire class. At the end of class, I began unplugging equipment near my bag but had not touched it. I glanced at my new treasure, and suddenly the owl balloon freed herself from the ribbon; she had just enough helium left in her to float without the weight of that darn leash! She drifted back up to the ceiling, the ribbon still tied tightly to my purse strap. I thought at that moment, *How perfect; I guess she was never really mine to keep or bring home.* She came through me but not to be with us on this plane of reality for very long. I held onto the ribbon, though, and it is still tied to my purse. I like to hold onto those little reminders that keep our relationship alive. I don't have her, but I have our relationship, and that will never die.

Seven pregnancies and two live births, I fought for my babies to be here, and my babies fought to be here—for the life we have built, and to cling to dreams of the impossible, even when my mind can't see the way through.

Every day, my girls teach me that riding the wings of hope and intuition will take us all further than any thinking can ever do.

About the Author

As a mommapreneur, I parent and work from my heart, which speaks through my intuition. I love being awed by stories of hope, success, and perseverance of the human spirit that fuel my belief in magic. Whether I am helping a client move through trauma, coaching a leader to create more successful interactions with employees, or nurturing an artist to get their work out there, I am living my dharma. I have a Master's degree in Mental Health Counseling, and a Master's degree in Industrial/Organizational Psychology, with training in Somatic Psychotherapy from Naropa University.

www.ingramcontent.com/pod-product-compliance
Lightning Source LLC
Chambersburg PA
CBHW012040140726

47991CB00011B/3212